SALMON COUNTRY

OTHER BOOKS BY ROBERT H. BUSCH

Wolf Songs: The Classic Collection of Writing about Wolves

The Wolf Almanac

The Cougar Almanac

Gray Whales, Wandering Giants

Valley of the Grizzlies

Loons

On Otter Pond

Salmon Country

A History of the Pacific Salmon

Robert H. Busch

KEY PORTER BOOKS

Canadian Cataloguing in Publication Data

Busch, Robert, 1953-
  Salmon country

ISBN 1-55263-162-1

1. Pacific salmon. I. Title.

QL638.S2B87 1999   587.5′6   C99-931102-6

The Canada Council | Le Conseil des Arts
FOR THE ARTS | DU CANADA
SINCE 1957 | DEPUIS 1957

The publisher gratefully acknowledges the assistance of the Canada Council and the
Ontario Arts Council.

Canadä

We acknowledge the financial support of the Government of Canada through the Book
Publishing Industry Development Program (BPIDP) for our publishing activities.

Key Porter Books Limited
70 The Esplanade
Toronto, Ontario
Canada M5E 1R2

www.keyporter.com

Electronic formatting: Jean Lightfoot Peters
Design: Peter Maher

00 01 02 03 6 5 4 3 2 1

For Duke, my best friend, missed and loved

CONTENTS

PREFACE

I saw my first salmon run in 1971 in a small stream north of Juneau, in Alaska. I'd read about these runs before, but nothing could have prepared me for the sight of a stream blushed pink by thousands of salmon struggling valiantly to return to the particular patch of gravel where they began their lives.

The annual migration of the salmon—one of the world's greatest wildlife wonders—ranks as a must-see for the growing numbers of people starved for the sight of natural marvels in an increasingly high-tech world.

Sadly the annual salmon runs are a quickly disappearing sight in a landscape wincing from the heavy blows of humankind. The tiny stream that thrilled me so some twenty years ago no longer harbors any salmon at all; it is a victim of the runaway clearcutting that has left a checkerboard of destruction across the Pacific Northwest.

Here in my home province of British Columbia, however, there are still dozens of streams that run red with salmon each fall. Just a short hike away from many of these streams are the remains of Native pit-houses, ancient shelters that were dug into the ground in order to protect their owners from the cruel Canadian winters. These dwellings were dug close to streams simply because the salmon was to the woodland Native people what the buffalo was to the plains Native people: the very fuel of life itself. In fact, many tribes referred to themselves simply and honestly as "Salmon People."

The coastal tribe of Kwakiutl, who depended heavily upon the salmon for their livelihood, celebrated the arrival of the fish each year with the unique "First Salmon Ceremony." It was during this annual ceremony that they would sing "O Supernatural Ones, O Swimmers, I thank you that you are willing to come to us ... you come to be food for us." The salmon was a symbol of wealth and prosperity to the Kwakiutl, and subsequently the killer whale, one of the few animals smart enough to be able to catch salmon for food, was deemed by the Kwakiutl to be a model fisher.

Other tribes also respected the salmon's contribution to their well-being. In British Columbia, the coastal Squamish, for example, believe that after a feast, each and every salmon bone must be returned to the sea, whereupon the fish reassemble themselves around the bones. And, in Japan, the Ainu people call the salmon simply and accurately "a present from heaven."

When the explorer Alexander Mackenzie reached the British Columbia coast in 1793, becoming the first European to traverse the northern part of the continent from Alberta over the mountains, the local Native people asked that he not use his iron kettle. They believed its strange smell would drive the salmon from the river. Such was the respect the aboriginal people showed to the fish that sustained their lives.

Many a modern fisher feels the same kind of deep respect for the noble salmon. There is something awesome about a fish that can tip the scales at 100 pounds (45 kg) and can swim over 3,000 miles (4,800 km) just to return to the place of its birth. And there is something very challenging about a fish that refuses to eat on its long migration home: for nearly 1 million sport anglers each year, there is quite simply no finer chase.

It was approximately 30,000 years ago that the first fishing hook was made, in southern Europe, fashioned from a piece of bone. The word *angler* actually derives from the Middle English word for hook, *angelen*. (This coincidence makes anglers the first happy hookers!)

Fishing has indeed been a part of life for centuries. The first written description of flyfishing was by Claudius Aelianus, in 300 B.C. He described people fishing with hooks that were fashioned from bits of wool and cock feathers, a combination that would still attract many salmon today.

According to most authorities, the first modern book on fishing was Dame Juliana Berner's *Treatyse of Fysshynge With an Angle*, published in 1496. The book recommended twelve kinds of artificial flies, ten of which are still in use. Five hundred years later, our fascination with fish and fishing continues; it is especially intense as we continue to learn more about the incredible migrations of spawning salmon.

One of the earliest known salmon fans was Izaac Walton, whose book *The Compleat Angler* has become a bible for anglers everywhere. Walton, a retired ironmonger, would have been shocked at the ripples his humble little book created; he didn't even put his name on the first edition. However, in the last 200 years, more than 300 editions of his book have been published worldwide.

The subtitle of Walton's book, *The Contemplative Man's Recreation*, is an apt description indeed, for only a thinking person can truly appreciate the silvery beauty of salmon flashing through Pacific waters, or the moving spectacle of creeks brimming with bright red salmon desperately trying to spawn before death takes them.

Although not all naturalists are anglers, I believe all good anglers are naturalists. This book is for good anglers everywhere.

ROBERT H. BUSCH

A nineteenth century engraving by A.B. Frost of an avid angler.

1. THE SPIRIT OF THE PACIFIC

"Man is not much good at helping the fish, but he is learning slowly."
RODERICK HAIG-BROWN, *Return to the River*, 1974

I live in salmon country. Just one valley east of me is perhaps the most famous of all salmon spawning grounds—the Adams River. Its gravel bed has been called the most valuable real estate in British Columbia due to the rich crop of sockeye salmon that spawns there each year. It is a treasure that must be preserved.

The Adams River is located about 40 miles (64 km) east of Kamloops, B.C., more than 300 miles (480 km) from the Pacific Ocean. The river is only 7 miles (11 km) long, and empties into Shuswap Lake, a popular recreation spot for both young humans and young sockeye salmon.

The Adams River was named for a Native chief, Sel-howt-ken, who in 1849 was renamed "Adam" by an overeager Oblate missionary. Unfortunately, the arrival of European settlers in 1862 brought not only new names to the Native people, but new diseases as well. "Adam," as well as hundreds of other Indians, later died of smallpox brought in by the settlers.

Today, the Adams River valley is protected as the Roderick Haig-Brown Provincial Park, named after one of the first author-anglers, Roderick Haig-Brown (1908–1976), who spoke out for the conservation of salmon waters at a time when resource exploitation was running rampant.

The dwindling numbers of salmon spawning in the Adams River in the early years have mirrored that exploitation. In the early 1900s, the Adams River was used for log drives, and at one point the damage wreaked by these drives caused the runs of sockeye to completely die out. The drives were stopped in 1922 and it was only then that the sockeyes were able to return and give the river a second chance. By 1934, the Adams run had rejuvenated enough to become the dominant run in the entire Fraser River system, but once again habitat loss and overfishing took a toll. By 1964, the sockeye run in the Adams River had shrunk again, this time to a pathetic 716 fish, barely enough for the stock to survive. Once again, after years of careful management the stocks have returned, so that now 1 million to 2.6 million sockeye spawn there every year. Painstakingly guarded by Fisheries biologists, the sockeye eggs laid in the gravel of the Adams River now have a successful hatch rate of 70 to 90 percent.

A number of other salmon stocks also spawn in the Adams River. These stocks include coho, chinook and pinks, but the star of the show remains the sockeye.

The sockeye runs in the Adams River peak every four years, for reasons that are still largely unknown. In these dominant years, the Adams run is the biggest of all sockeye runs in British Columbia. The next dominant run isn't expected until 2002.

In autumn, the Adams River valley is suffused in an explosion of color. Tones of amber, cinnamon and burnt orange dapple the poplars that stoop over the river like tired old men. Gentle breezes stir the dying leaves; to unsuspecting tourists and poetic writers, it sounds like the salmon are sighing. Feathery cedars in coats of green and rusty brown attest to the moist richness of the valley's climate. The trees shading the river cool the water to just the right temperature for spawning salmon. The water is so cold that it bites back when you sip it. Widespread gravel beds provide an excellent medium for salmon nests, and nearby Shuswap Lake provides a deep, cool nursery for sockeye fry. It is the perfect habitat for salmon.

Every October, hordes of people walk slowly and reverently

along the well-marked paths that line the river's edge. There is little talk; everybody knows they are there to witness something special and rare. The hush is reminiscent of the awe experienced in a magnificent cathedral. To local merchants, the event is equally exciting: the 100,000-plus tourists that descend upon the area each year infuse capital into the area, prompting local tourist boards to stage an annual glitzy "Salute to the Sockeye."

In the river, thousands of gaudy red salmon can be seen crowding the cold, clear water. Their red backs often appear above the water's surface, prompting a young boy to ask his father if the fish were sunburned. Sometimes the salmon are barely visible among the ripples and waves of the water's surface; their shimmering images suggest an almost ethereal presence in the water.

The fiercely distorted faces of the male sockeye lend an aggressive, almost prehistoric air to the valley. Occasionally a fight between two male salmon will boil the waters and elicit gasps from the human audience. Park interpreters stand patiently in front of eager groups of tourists, answering the same questions over and over again: "How come they're so red?" "What kind of salmon is this?"

The Adams run is more than a tourist attraction; it represents one of the few opportunities for people to observe a miracle of nature, a sight that, in return, often inspires an appropriate feeling of humility.

In more material terms, though, the Adams run is one of the most lucrative fishing resources on the continent. Perhaps Alan Haig-Brown, the son of Roderick Haig-Brown, was correct when he wrote, "the word *resource* doesn't do them justice; salmon are the unifying *spirit* of all the Pacific."[1]

When referring to salmon, the word *spirit* may be appropriate for another reason. The millions of salmon that manage to complete the miraculous journey each fall to their original spawning grounds are one of the last examples of wildlife that once existed so plentifully in North America. It is estimated that the buffalo, for example, which once covered the Western plains, numbered in the hundreds of millions. Today, buffalo exist only in a few preserves and game ranches. The great grizzly bear also used to range from the state of California as far east as Minnesota. Today,

The Spirit of the Pacific

99 percent of the grizzly population in the lower forty-eight states has been completely wiped out. The passenger pigeon, great auk, sea mink, Steller's sea cow and dozens of other species have similarly disappeared from the earth forever. Their spirits haunt us, reminding us that, in the world of wildlife, there is no safety in numbers.

The salmon act as a kind of natural barometer; they measure the well-being of the Pacific Ocean. Their strong and abundant presence is a sign that all is well in the ecological world of water. Their decline, on the other hand, acts as a warning to humans that something (i.e., humankind) has damaged the water's delicate balance.

Part of the problem is that it has taken us far too long to realize that the millions of salmon in our waters are as precious a natural resource as the forests and minerals that make our continent one of the richest sources for natural resources on this planet. The salmon's presence has been taken for granted for so long, and so little effort has been expended toward its conservation that now it is virtually too late. The huge salmon fisheries of the past were once a source of national pride on both sides of the Canada–U.S. border; today, the collapse of this fishery is an international disgrace.

As I write these words, the Fraser River sockeye fishery, the richest on the continent, has been closed to both commercial and recreational fishing because stock levels are dangerously low. Some conservationists believe that even this drastic move may be a case of "too little too late": independent Fisheries consultant David Ellis has called for an immediate four-year ban on all commercial salmon fishing in order to attempt to rebuild the stocks. Across North America, many salmon streams can now be fished legally only by catch-and-release anglers, in a desperate last-ditch attempt to preserve the salmon resource. But one wonders if this kind of back-and-forthing is really an effective conservation method.

Ironically, the problems now faced by the salmon come at a time when the demand for the fish is at an all-time high. Many people watching their diets are switching from high-fat meats—beef, pork and lamb—to low-fat alternatives such as chicken and fish. Of all the fish to choose from, salmon provide an impressive list of health benefits. It has been found, for example, that a once-a-week serving of salmon can decrease the risk of coronary heart disease by up to 50 percent. The agents responsible for this are omega-3 fatty acids and one of the richest sources of these acids is salmon meat. Recently research has found that people who have low levels of omega-3 fatty acids have a higher risk of developing depression. There also appears to be a direct link between countries where salmon is a dietary staple (such as Japan and South Korea) and lower rates of depression. Furthermore, it has been found that a weekly serving of salmon can dramatically reduce the risk of stroke and lower the incidence of diabetes—clearly a strong case for increasing salmon consumption.

Although none of the six North American salmon species is in immediate danger of extinction, many of the individual stocks are likely doomed to disappear. (A stock is a group of fish of one species that share a common spawning ground.) According to the U.S. Fish and Wildlife Service, almost half of the Columbia River basin stocks are threatened with extinction. The Red Fish Lake sockeye in Idaho, for example, is so rare that in 1998 only one fish returned to the spawning grounds. Biologists captured the fish and froze its sperm in the unlikely event that a female would show up someday and they would be able to rejuvenate the stocks. The scientists have dubbed the fish "Lonely Leo."

In the early 1990s, approximately 100 salmon stocks in the United States have become extinct. According to a 1993 U.S. Fish and Wildlife Service study, 90 percent of the remaining 200-plus salmon stocks in the Pacific Northwest have been deemed to be at risk of extinction. Stocks in Alaska are generally regarded as healthy; of the 900 Alaskan salmon stocks recently identified by the American Fisheries Society, only 37 appear to be on the decline.

In British Columbia, 142 salmon stocks have gone extinct since 1950, out of a total 5,508 stocks studied. Another 624 stocks are at a high risk of extinction, threatened by a combination of overfishing and habitat loss. Some of these stocks have sunk to such low levels that extinction is virtually guaranteed: the Kauwich run on Vancouver Island, for example, has declined to a mere four fish.

Steelhead numbers have been especially hard hit; since reaching a peak in 1984, steelhead counts have shown steady declines across North America, primarily due to habitat loss.

One hundred years ago, anglers from all over the country would come to try their luck in the famed Trinity River in California. Today the main-stem Trinity steelhead probably number fewer than 100. Steelhead runs in the Columbia River are now at about a third of historical levels; the number of steelhead returning to the Wells Dam in 1995 was among the lowest ever on record. On July 30, 1996, the National Marine Fisheries Service announced that almost all of the steelhead stocks in the lower forty-eight states will likely be listed as either threatened or endangered, due to vastly dwindling numbers. Since that announcement, the lower California steelhead stock and two others have already made the endangered list.

In British Columbia, the number of steelhead on spawning beds in the Thompson River peaked at 10,000 in 1985. Today, fewer than 1,500 fish use those same beds.

The steelhead isn't doing any better in Asia either, and in

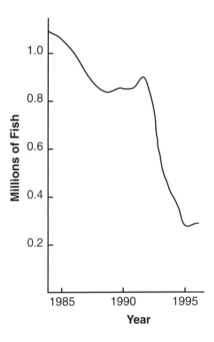

FIGURE 1. Canadian commercial and recreational chinook catch, 1985–1997. (Source: Department of Fisheries and Oceans)

Russia it is listed in the *Red Book of Rare and Disappearing Species*.

Also hard hit is the chinook salmon, the rarest and most sought-after game fish in the salmon family. Since the early 1970s, chinook numbers have been in a general decline. The

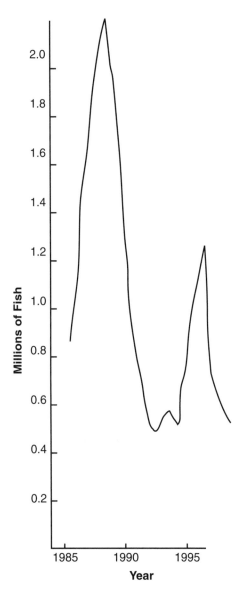

FIGURE 2. California, Oregon and Washington ocean commercial troll and recreational chinook catch, 1985–1998. (Source: Pacific Fishery Management Council)

Canadian commercial catch is now a fifth of what it was only a decade ago. The Puntledge River on Vancouver Island has also shown a typical decline; in 1997, only 315 summer-run chinook and 333 fall-run chinook returned to the river to spawn, less than 10 percent of historical levels. The 1996 chinook catch in Canada was the lowest on record, only a sixth of the peak 1971 catch (see Figure 1). The 1996 chinook catch in Washington, California and Oregon was less than half the peak 1988 catch (see Figure 2).

Although coho stocks in Alaska are thriving, their situation in the lower forty-eight states is a real sob story, with populations down between 90 and 95 percent of historical levels. As recently as the 1940s, California had runs that numbered in the range of 500,000 cohos annually; only a few thousand exist today. Oregon used to produce millions of cohos each year; that number is now down to about 50,000. In Washington's Puget Sound, the coho population has declined by 75 percent. The National Marine Fisheries Service has recommended that all coho stocks in central and northern California, southern Oregon, northern Oregon and

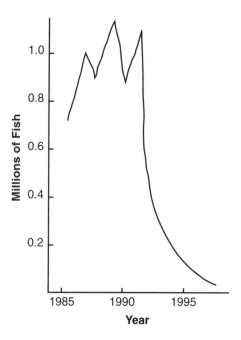

FIGURE 3. California, Oregon and Washington ocean commercial troll and recreational coho catch, 1985–1998. (Source: Pacific Fishery Management Council)

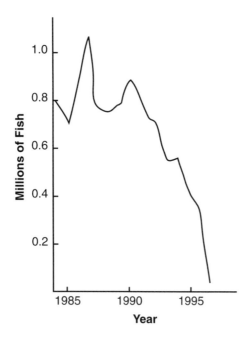

FIGURE 4. Canadian commercial and recreational coho catch, 1985–1997. (Source: Department of Fisheries and Oceans)

the lower Columbia region be classed as threatened. The coho catch in Washington, Oregon and California peaked in 1971 at over 4 million fish; by 1997, the catch had shrunk to a shocking 45,000 (see Figure 3).

The coho catches in British Columbia used to be truly phenomenal. British Columbia's catches of wild coho have declined by an average of 66,000 fish annually for the past fifteen years. The province used to report coho in nearly 2,000 streams; today, they are present in only 128. The decline in the Babine Lake coho population is typical: from an average population of 20,000 to 100,000 spawners in the mid-1960s, numbers have plummeted to only 469 in 1997. The 1996 coho catch in Canada was the lowest on record, less than a third of the peak 1986 catch (see Figure 4). The closing of the Canadian commercial coho fishery in 1998 is the strongest indication of this sorry state of affairs.

By early 1999, it became obvious that the Pacific salmon were in big trouble. In March, the U.S. National Marine Fisheries Service added nine salmon runs to the endangered/threatened list under the U.S. Endangered Species Act. These nine salmon runs

The Spirit of the Pacific

are all in Washington and Oregon: the Puget Sound chinook, Lower Columbia River spring chinook, Upper Columbia River spring chinook, Lake Ozette sockeye, Hood Canal summer chum, Lower Columbia River chum, Mid-Columbia River steelhead, and Upper Willamette River steelhead and chinook. In announcing the new listings, U.S. Assistant Commerce Secretary Terry Garcia said pointedly that "people need to ask [themselves] whether they want to be the last generation in the Northwest to have the privilege of marvelling at these wild stocks of salmon. You can choose to send these species along the path to extinction or choose to find a path that will allow you to take them with us into the next millennium."[2]

In Canada, there is still no federal endangered species act, a disgraceful situation that is condemned by conservationists across the country. In fact, the province of British Columbia has actually opposed proposed federal endangered species legislation, fearing it would lead to lost jobs in the fishing and forestry sectors, and knowing that lost jobs could mean lost votes in the next election.

Canada has in fact lagged sadly behind the United States with respect to most facets of salmon conservation. Only in the past decade has the Canadian federal Department of Fisheries and Oceans reacted strongly to the decline of the salmon resource, the equivalent of waiting until the floodwater is up to your neck before sticking your finger in the dike. It was not until July 1998 that David Anderson, then Minister of Fisheries and Oceans, finally admitted, "It's time to admit that we've made mistakes, and begin the hard work of correcting them."[3]

Unfortunately, many of these corrections have had their human costs. One of the biggest challenges in resource management today, whether that resource be trees, minerals or fish, is balancing conservation of the resource with the welfare of the people involved in taking that resource. In the case of the Pacific salmon fishery, putting fish first often results in the loss of jobs and economic hardship for fishers and fishing-based communities.

In recent years, salmon fishers have been hit by a combination punch of declining prices, dwindling stocks and tough fishing restrictions. The price of wild salmon has dropped dramatically in recent years, as farmed Atlantic and coho salmon have flooded the

market, and wild salmon stocks have hit all-time lows. Never
before have salmon fishers been affected by so many layers of legislation in their pursuit of the fish.

It is very difficult to quantify just how many fishers have left
the business as a result of each of these factors, and even more
difficult to predict the future of the situation. All it would take is
one change in elected government—state, provincial or federal—
to produce sweeping changes in fisheries policy, with long-reach-
ing effects.

However, the human costs in recent years have been sizable. In
British Columbia alone, between March 1996 and March 1999, a
total of 1,555 salmon fishers voluntarily sold their fishing licenses
back to the government and left the business. The effect on small
fishing communities has been devastating. According to one estimate, 29 percent of all jobs in the tiny fishing town of Kyuquot, on
Vancouver Island, were lost in one year due to federal fishing policies. The Sports Fishing Institute estimates that, as a result of
coho fishing closures, business in 1998 dropped off by 40 percent
for fishing-related businesses on both sides of the border in the
Strait of Georgia, ranging from direct fishing losses to indirect
reductions in tackle, fuel and accommodation expenses.

In many areas, the salmon fisher has become just as endangered as the salmon.

The story of the decline of the Pacific salmon is a long and
involved one, with tragic elements of overfishing, habitat loss, climate change, fisheries mismanagement, and a dozen other inter-
connected factors. But to fully understand the collapse of the
fisheries, you must first understand the fish itself.

2. A FAMILY OF FISH

"Little salmons...abound in many rivers relating to the sea."
IZAAC WALTON, *The Compleat Angler*, 1653

One of my favorite works of art, that sits on my living room wall, is a framed fossil fish from the Green River shales of Wyoming. I admire this fossil fish not only for its esthetic appeal, but also for the clear image it evokes of a fish dating from 50 million years ago. The bones of this prehistoric fossil fish make it easy for me to mentally plaster on muscle and flesh and so reconstruct the fish itself. Similarly, the many bones of the salmon's skeleton have made it easier for paleontologists to reconstruct its evolution in some detail.

SALMON EVOLUTION
The earliest known fish fossils are actually only tiny chips of armor taken from the external skeleton of a jawless fish that prowled the seas during the Middle Ordovician Period (see Appendix A), about 460 million years ago. This fish was one of the first members of the class Pisces, the group to which all fish belong. Today, there are more than 20,000 species of fish; they now outnumber, by a ratio of twenty to one, all other classes of vertebrates put together.

Thirty million years after the Ordovician Period came the Devonian Period, also known as the Age of Fish. During this time, the ancient seas were filled with a myriad of bizarre armored and fanged fish.

Early fish from the Devonian Period either were soft-bodied or had a hard external carapace similar to that of modern lobsters. The first truly bony fish to appear in the fossil record evolved approximately 190 million years ago.

We tend to take internal skeletons for granted since they are a part of our own anatomy, but consider the advantages of an internal skeleton to the early bony fish. With an internal skeleton bony fish could flex their bodies, a definite advantage to speed and agility when swimming through a watery medium. An internal skeleton also provided an anchor for the muscles used in swimming, in addition to helping protect sensitive internal organs.

The evolution of fins was also a major breakthrough for fish; the earliest fish were bottom dwellers that could only crawl along the ocean floor, seeking food. Fins provided extra maneuverability, and this aided in chasing prey and evading predators. One scientific theory suggests that fins developed as a result of overcrowding and increased competition for food along the ocean floor. Most likely, fins evolved from the flaps of skin found between the spines of ancient fish; as the spines degenerated and gradually disappeared, the flaps of skin evolved into fins.

Both salmon and trout are members of the Salmonidae family. The Salmonidae family first appeared during the Cretaceous Period, approximately 144 million years ago. The oldest known fossil salmonid, *Eosalmo driftwoodensis*, lived in Eocene freshwater lakes approximately 55 million years ago. Another prehistoric salmonid, *Smilodonichthys rastrosus*, was almost 10 feet (3 m) long—a length that would make any modern angler drool.

Approximately 30 million years ago, the salmon subfamily had evolved, creating the genus we now call *Salmo*. Since then the salmon's story depends on which biologist you believe—although the salmon family tree has strong roots, its branches are pretty shaky.

Some biologists believe that Pacific salmon evolved from the early *Salmo* fish that ranged through the Atlantic Ocean. When the Bering Land Bridge (a land bridge that connected Asia with North America) rose about 10 million years ago, it was believed the fish were cut off from the Atlantic Ocean and thus gradually evolved into seven new species. This was a neat theory, but it suffered a major setback when fossils of Pacific salmon were recently found in California and Nevada in deposits that were at least 20 million years old.

Some biologists have now reverted to an earlier theory that suggests that the Pacific salmon's ancestor was a marine fish that originated in the Sea of Japan, and not in the Atlantic Ocean.

Still other biologists believe that the early *Salmo* ancestor was not a marine fish at all, but a stream or lake inhabitant. These biologists point out that salmon almost always reproduce in fresh water, and that this fact therefore suggests a freshwater origin. The fact that no wholly marine salmon exist today also suggests a freshwater ancestor. Additionally, freshwater supporters use the existence of permanently freshwater forms of masu, kokanee and Atlantic salmon as evidence of their theory. Biologists also point out that lampreys, sharks and other fish believed to have evolved in the ocean have no air bladders, since they are unnecessary in the buoyant salty ocean. Salmon, on the other hand, *do* have air bladders, a fact that also suggests a freshwater origin.

If you believe in the marine origin theory, the first Pacific salmon to evolve was the masu salmon, followed by the steelhead, coho, chinook, sockeye, chum and pink. Those who believe in the freshwater origin reverse this list. Whatever the order, the last Pacific species to evolve may have appeared as recently as 500,000 years ago.

Clearly, much remains to be learned about the evolutionary history of Pacific salmon. Current research into the DNA tracing of salmon, however, may solve the question of their origin once and for all.

All salmon are anadromous, a ten-dollar word which simply means they spend a part of their lives in salt water and return to fresh water to spawn. The word *anadromous* is derived from the Greek *ana*, meaning "up," and *dromein*, meaning "to run." Anadromous fish are therefore those fish that run up streams in order to spawn. Other anadromous fish include some whitefish, char and trout. Biologists believe that the evolution of anadromous fish from saltwater fish began about 1 million years ago, when abundant meltwater from retreating glaciers entered the oceans and lowered its salinity, forcing fish to adapt in order to survive.

Today, members of the Salmonidae family are the dominant freshwater fish of the northern hemisphere—the most successful family of fish in North America.

SALMON HABITAT

According to a Haida legend, the Raven brought all the lakes and streams of the Haida islands to the area in its beak during the time of Creation. And it was in the waters of those lakes and streams that the salmon lay. As the legend goes, "That's why today nearly every one of the Haida islands is splattered with little lakes and... streams [full of salmon], some of which still provide welcome meals for the Raven and all his relations." Unfortunately, many other lakes and streams across North America aren't as lucky as to have this abundant cache of salmon in their waters.

As any angler knows, each salmon species tends to prefer a particular habitat and to live within a more or less defined range. In fishing lingo, the angler's secret is to know how to look for the right fish in the right place.

Generally speaking fish are incredibly sensitive to water temperature. Pacific salmon in particular prefer cold water and are most comfortable in water that would set a human's teeth chattering—53 to 57°F (12 to 14°C). Chinook and coho can survive in water that is a bit warmer than that tolerated by other species, but, for most salmon species, water above 75°F (24°C)—just where humans are comfortable—is lethal.

To a large degree, a fish's choice of water is dependent on the amount of oxygen in the water, which, in turn, is dependent upon the water's temperature. If all other things are equal, cold water holds more oxygen than warm water. At 32°F (0°C), a body of water can hold about 66 percent more oxygen than it can at 68°F (20°C).

As a cold-blooded species, a salmon's body temperature and oxygen demand increase with a rise in water temperature. The warmer the water, the more oxygen is required by the salmon. The normal range of oxygen required in water is about 6 to 10 parts per million. When water temperatures suddenly rise, the

A Family of Fish

salmon's activity and oxygen demands increase until the oxygen content of the water can no longer meet the level required for the body's metabolism and then the fish slowly dies. When water temperatures suddenly cool, salmon become sluggish and are slow to feed. At temperatures below 39°F (4°C), most salmon will refuse to spawn.

During prolonged heat waves, salmon will often move to cleaner or faster-moving water, where oxygen from the air is mixed into the water through turbulence. During the scorching summer of 1994, the water temperature in the main branch of the Fraser River approached 68°F (20°C), the warmest recorded temperature since 1942. An estimated 500,000 fish died as a result. When Mount St. Helens blew its top in 1980, salmon in the Cowlitz River literally leapt out of the river in order to prevent being scalded by water temperatures that soared above 90°F (32°C).

The general rule in looking for salmon, then, is to look for clean, cold water in streams deep enough not to dry up or heat up during long hot summers. Streams meeting these requirements vary widely, from nameless tiny trickles to huge roaring rivers. All are part of salmon country.

SALMON TAXONOMY AND DESCRIPTION

The six Pacific salmon species found in North America have scientific names that are a mix of Latin and Russian, a bizarre situation caused by a quirk of history.

The names were given by Georg Wilhelm Steller (1709–1746), a German naturalist employed by the St. Petersburg Academy of Sciences. Steller explored much of the North Pacific on behalf of the Russian government, traveling as a naturalist on the 1737 expedition to Alaska led by Vitus Jonassen Bering. The members of this expedition were the first white men to land in that region. On the return voyage, the expedition was storm-wrecked off Bering Island, a barren chunk of sand just off the Kamchatka Peninsula. Vitus Bering himself died there in 1741, but Steller and a few others survived by relying heavily upon the salmon that appeared in the streams during the spring.

For the next three years, Steller roamed the Kamchatkan and Siberian hills, studying for the first time their rich natural history.

The Steller's sea cow, jay, eider, eagle and white raven were all named for this pioneer naturalist of the Pacific. He was also the first to identify the separate salmon species, giving them species names from the Kamchatka Peninsula dialect. Steller escaped from the island in 1742, but died four years later, in 1746, at the age of thirty-seven. An associate, Stefan P. Kracheninnikov, used Steller's notes and journals to write a natural history of Kamchatka in 1755. Kracheninnikov's book, published in English in 1764, was the first comprehensive volume on the Pacific salmon.

All Pacific salmon belong to the genus *Oncorhynchus*, which is a Latin term for "hook-nosed," in reference to the kype, or hook, that develops on the upper jaw of some male Pacific salmon during the spawning season.

All Pacific salmon also share dark backs and light bellies. This shading provides excellent camouflage from predators both above and below. The lustrous silvery color on the flanks is caused by the reflection of light in the tiny guanine crystals that make up the fish's scales. The scales lie embedded in the fish's skin at an angle, and overlap one another just like tiles on a roof. The leading edge of the scales points to the rear of the fish, so water flows over the scales smoothly and evenly, like rain running from a tiled roof.

Salmon have two layers of skin: an outer epidermis that covers the scales, and a thicker inner skin that contains the color pigments. At spawning time, these color pigments are responsible for some of the flashiest coats in all of the animal kingdom.

The seven salmon species have been given a myriad of monickers. The most commonly used names are chinook, steelhead, chum, coho, pink, sockeye and masu.

To pioneer angler Izaac Walton, the mighty salmon was deserving of another more regal name. He called the salmon simply "the King of freshwater fish."

Chinook salmon

The chinook salmon, *Oncorhynchus tshawytscha*, is the giant of the family, named after the Chinook Natives who once lived along the Columbia River. The term *tyee* (a Native word meaning "chief") is often used for chinook salmon weighing more than 30 pounds (13 kg). Chinooks are also known as kings, blackmouths, hogs, chubs, hookbills, smileys, sea trout and pigs. In Alaska they are known by a Native name: quinnats. In California, they are known as Sacramentos, after the river in which they once flourished.

Chinooks have the typical salmon appearance: silver sides and white bellies, with green-blue-black backs. They have irregular black spots along their backs, dorsal fins and both lobes of the tail fin. With numerous needle-like teeth, chinooks are considered the wolves of the salmon family.

Chinooks may be distinguished from the equally toothy coho by their spotted lower tail-fin lobes and by their dark-colored lower gums (which have led to their nickname "blackmouths"). In addition, chinooks have a particularly musky odor.

Unlike most salmon, chinooks do not undergo drastic physical changes during the spawning season. Their color merely changes from silver to a dark gray-brown, and the males grow a little in size. Their flesh may be white, pink or red, the red flesh having the most commercial value.

Chinooks are considered the giants of the salmon family and the stuff of legends, averaging 36 inches (91 cm) in length and 20 to 50 pounds (9 to 23 kg) in weight. Anglers catch chinooks by trolling with herring or with artificial lures attached to flashers. One of the most popular chinook lures is the "hootchie," or imitation squid.

The largest chinook on record is a 126.5-pound (57.5-kg) monster taken by a commercial angler near Petersburg, Alaska, in 1959; this super salmon was over 4 feet (1.5 m) long. There is an undocumented record of a 102-pound (46.3-kg) chinook gaffed from the Elwha River in Washington. The all-tackle world record is a 97.2-pound (44.2-kg) fish taken in 1985 from Alaska's famed Kenai River. A number of other chinooks in the 80-to-95-pound (36-to-40-kg) range have been taken by anglers in the Skeena River and Rivers Inlet areas of British Columbia.

Chinook salmon can be found in large streams from the Ventura River in central California north to Point Hope in Alaska, with reports of chinook in the Coppermine River, even further east on the Arctic coast. In 1983 a single specimen was collected from the Liard River in the upper Mackenzie River drainage. At one time, runs existed as far south as San Diego. Hatchery runs now exist in California's San Joaquin system, and transplanted populations exist in the Great Lakes, to the delight of avid Eastern anglers.

In Asia, chinook range from the Japanese island of Hokkaido north to the Anadyr River.

Chinook were transplanted to New Zealand around the turn of the century, and can now be found in many rivers along the east coast of the South Island and some rivers on the West Coast.

Chinook are the least abundant of Pacific salmon, which is ironic since they are the largest of salmon and a prized game fish. They also tend to travel the least distance into the oceans and are usually found north of 50°N latitude. Chinooks are deep-water fish; during migration they like to travel in water that is 70 to 120 feet (21 to 37 m) deep, relatively close to shore. Occasionally, they go to even greater depths; commercial trawlers have caught chinook at depths greater than 1,500 feet (457 m). Unlike many other salmon, they do not swim in tight schools. Chinook are loners.

Of all the salmon, chinook and coho are the two species most likely to take a fly or baited hook in salt water. At spawning time, chinooks tend to prefer major rivers rather than small streams.

Well-known sport-fishing spots for chinook include the Campbell River in British Columbia and the Kenai River in Alaska. It is a fishing axiom that if you want to find lots of salmon, just look for lots of anglers. Nowhere is this more true than the Kenai—I once counted more than a hundred anglers lining its banks, elbow to elbow. I am told that the nearest camping sites must now be booked at least a year in advance.

Steelhead salmon

The steelhead salmon is known to scientists as *Oncorhynchus mykiss*. Steelheads were classed for years as *Salmo gairdneri*, or Gairdner's trout (after Dr. Meredith Gairdner, an early naturalist with the Hudson's Bay Company). In 1989, however, the American Society of Ichthyologists, after additional intensive study of the fish's anatomy and behavior, officially changed the steelhead's Latin name.

In fishing slang, steelheads are known as steelies, hardheads, metalheads, ironheads, salmon trout and coastal rainbows. Anglers use the term "bright steelies" for fish newly arrived from the ocean; "dark steelies" are those steelheads caught at spawning time. A race of steelheads indigenous only to the Rogue River in Oregon and Klamath River in California are known as half-pounders. These fish return to the rivers after less than a year at sea and are always pint-sized. Pacific coastal Native people call steelheads "little salmon," a term which, unfortunately, is also used for kokanees. Rainbow trout are a landlocked form of steelhead.

Steelhead have tail fins that look like a Chinese fan made up of radiating black lines. They have a distinctive pinkish band along their sides, especially well developed in spawning males. (This band has led to their land-locked kin being called "rainbows.") The head is relatively short compared with total body length, and the forehead is gunmetal blue—thus the name steelhead. The tail fin is square cut, and the anal fin is very short compared with that of other salmon. The interior of the mouth is white, which distinguishes steelhead from small chinook (which have a black mouth interior) and coho (whose mouths are grayish).

Steelhead average about 12 pounds (5 kg) in weight and 24 inches (61 cm) in length. The record steelhead appears to be a 47.5-pound (21.6-kg) fish netted from the Babine River in British Columbia. The sport record is a 42.1-pound (19.1-kg) fish from Bell Island, Alaska.

Steelhead can be found from Rio Santo Domingo in Baja California north to the Kuskokwim River in Alaska. In southern California, steelhead runs are only remnants of what they used to be, though, north of the Sacramento River, good steelhead runs still exist.

Steelhead were first introduced into the Great Lakes in the early twentieth century, using transplants from the famed McCloud River in California. Today, biologists estimate that steelhead runs in Lake Erie and Lake Ontario tributaries average between 10 and 15 percent wild fish; the rest are hatchery-bred.

In Asia, a related species can be found in the region of the Okhotsk Sea and along the east coast of the Kamchatka Peninsula, home of both big bears and big salmon.

Steelhead prefer water of about 55°F (13°C), and are abundant in the Gulf of Alaska and along the western shore of North

America in waters between the 41 and 59°F (5 and 15°C) isotherms. In fresh water, steelhead prefer fast-moving water, and can be found in the rapids and riffles of rivers rather than the pools where the coho hide.

Steelhead are a prized game fish, first popularized by Zane Grey in his 1928 book *Tales of Freshwater Fishing*. Grey chased the mighty steelhead in California's famous Klamath and Rogue Rivers, where huge steelhead runs are now a thing of the past.

Today, many trophy steelhead come from the Babine and Skeena Rivers in British Columbia, and from a number of rivers in the United States: the Smith, Eel, Klamath, and Rogue (California); the Deschutes and Cowlitz (Oregon); and the Umpqua, Skykomish and Suislaw (Washington). The largest wild steelhead run in Alaska is in the Situk River, near Yakutat, in the southeast corner of the state.

Chum salmon

The chum salmon, *Oncorhynchus keta*, is the black sheep of the family. *Chum* is a word denoting any type of cheap bait fish, and its application to this species of salmon comes from its bland, poor-tasting flesh. It is widely known as dog salmon, after the fierce canine appearance of the breeding males. *Keta* is the Kamchatkan Russian word for "dog," although it also means "fish" in the Nanai dialect of Russia. Chum are also known as calico salmon and by the coastal Native names qualla, hayho and lekai. In Japan, late-running chum are called "gilas."

Chum are at the bottom of the barrel in terms of commercial value and visual appeal. They have small black specks on their backs, with faint grid-like bars running along their sides. The pectoral, anal and tail fins are also often edged in black, though they do change to white at spawning time. The chum's eyes have a large pupil, which is about half the total diameter of the eye.

During the spawning season, a wavy red streak or series of dark purplish vertical bars develops along the side of the chum's body. Spawning males also develop larger front teeth than other salmon species, giving them a fierce, dog-like appearance.

Chum flesh is yellowish, bland and poor-tasting, due largely to its low fat content. It is used mostly as dog food in northern regions, although it is popular human fare in Japan and the Far East. Much of the sushi that tourists nibble on in Tokyo and Hong Kong is actually made from chum salmon. Pickled chum roe, called "sujiko," is a popular Oriental dish.

Adult chum average 25 inches (63 cm) in length and weigh less than 10 pounds (5 kg). Chum sometimes will take an artificial fly, but more commonly respond to trolled metal lures. The angling record for a chum is a 34.5-pound (15.6-kg) fish caught in Edye Pass near Prince Rupert, British Columbia, in 1995. There is an undocumented story of a 45.8-pound (20.8-kg) chum caught off Quadra Island, British Columbia, in 1928, but most biologists believe that this is yet another fish story.

Chum salmon range sporadically from the San Lorenzo River, in California, north to the Mackenzie River, in Canada's Northwest Territories, though occasionally a commercial ocean catch is made as far south as Del Mar, California. Small runs exist in the Sacramento and Klamath Rivers in California, and Tillamook Bay and Kilchis River in Oregon. The only state with large chum runs is Alaska; in British Columbia, only a dozen or so streams have large runs.

In Asia, chum range from Japan north to the Arctic Ocean and west along the northern edge of the Russian Federation to the Lena River. The major Asian chum spawning grounds are on the Russian mainland, from the Amur River to Olyutor, and on the islands of Sakhalin and Hokkaido. Historically, chum once ranged as far south as northeastern China.

For some reason, chum only occasionally take a lure, though they do put up a good fight when caught. In fact, many anglers give chum the title of the hardest-fighting salmon. (Although how much fighting can a 2-pound (1-kg) fish really do?)

One of the best angling spots for chum is off British Columbia's Queen Charlotte Islands. Chum physically deteriorate quickly upon spawning and therefore must be caught early in the season.

Coho salmon

The coho salmon, *Oncorhynchus kisutch*, is prized as both a commercial and a game fish. The word *coho* first appeared in print in 1878 as *co-hue*, apparently derived from either the Chilliwack and

Musqueam word for the fish, *kwahwult*, or from the Sooke and Saanich word *kuchuks*. Coho are also known as sea trout, hooknoses, dogs, jacks, silver salmon and bluebacks.

Coho look very similar to chinooks with silver sides, white bellies and green-blue-black backs, but have spots only on the upper lobes of their tail fins. In addition, their lower gums are light-colored. Many fishers believe that coho scales have a more silvery sheen than those of other salmon. At spawning time, the cohos' skin darken and their sides take on a reddish hue. Spawning males usually sport a red flank below the lateral line and are olive green on the back and head. Coho have a paler flesh than either chinook or sockeye.

Adult coho average 24 inches (61 cm) in length and 10 pounds (5 kg) in weight. Coho will take a wide variety of lures, including streamer flies and fly-and-spinner combinations trolled behind a fast-moving boat. The record Pacific coho catch is a 31.5-pound (14.3-kg) fish taken from Cowichan Bay on Vancouver Island in 1947. Coho have been transplanted to the Great Lakes, where a 33.25-pound (15.1-kg) hatchery-reared fish holds the Lakes record. To the dismay of flyfishing aficionados everywhere, the coho and the chinook are the only two Pacific salmon that will readily go after artificial flies.

Coho salmon range from Monterey Bay in California north to Point Hope in Alaska. Occasionally, stray coho can be found as far south as Chamalu Bay in Baja California. Fisheries biologists in both California and Oregon have transplanted coho into a number of artificial reservoirs, where they have become popular game fish. More than 50 million coho have been transplanted into the Great Lakes.

Asian coho range from Peter the Great Bay, on the mainland opposite Japan, north to the Anadyr River in the Russian Federation.

The North American coho catch is about twice the Asian catch. Most of the North American catch comes from British Columbia.

Coho are found closer to the surface than chinook, and therefore strike more often at artificial lures, leaping wildly when hooked. In fact, the word *salmon* comes from the Latin *salire*, meaning "to leap."

At sea, coho are most common in the central portion of their range, with populations tapering off to the north and south. Whereas chinook like to migrate relatively close to shore, coho prefer to stay from 1 to 3 miles (1.6 to 4.8 km) offshore. They swim in tight schools less than 50 feet (15 m) across and are easily spotted on fish-finders. Coho are very territorial fish; saltwater anglers look for coho in bays and coves, where the fish like to feed on herring and candlefish. Similarly, in fresh water they prefer to stay in deep pools. Coho rarely go far inland to spawn, preferring coastal streams.

Famous coho waters include the Klamath River (California), the Nehalem and Tillamook Rivers (Oregon), Puget Sound (Washington) and the Campbell River (British Columbia).

Pink salmon

The most common salmon is the pink, *Oncorhynchus gorbuscha*, named for the color of its flesh. Pinks are also known as humpbacks or humpies. *Gorbuscha* is the Kamchatkan Russian word for humpback.

Pinks have large black splotches nearly the size of their eyes along their backs and tail fins. These are the largest spots to be found on any Pacific salmon. Pinks have unusually small scales, and at spawning time the males develop an extremely humped back and a hooked upper jaw. Spawning males and females both develop a pink-brown stripe along their sides and pale pink-gray backs, but the females tend to have duller colors than the males. Commercial fishers call pinks "slimies," insisting they are the slimiest of all salmon.

In 1968, 150 albino pink fry were observed in Sashin Creek, Alaska, though none is believed to have survived to adulthood. (There is only one known record of a wild adult albino salmon.)

Pinks are small fish, averaging only 20 inches (50 cm) in length and weighing less than 5 pounds (3 kg). Although there is an unsubstantiated record of a 15-pound (16.8-kg) rod-caught pink, the largest documented catch is a 12.6-pound (5.7-kg) fish taken from the confluence of Alaska's Moose and Kenai Rivers in 1983. Because they usually only eat tiny plankton, pinks will rarely respond to anglers' lures.

Pink salmon are the sparrows of the salmon family, found everywhere and in great numbers. They range from La Jolla, California, all the way north to the Mackenzie River in the Northwest Territories. They are most common from Puget Sound north, with the largest runs occurring in Alaska.

In Asia, they range from Peter the Great Bay north to the Bering Sea, and west along the northern coast of the Russian Federation to the Lena River. Both the east and west coasts of the Kamchatka Peninsula support large runs of pinks.

One of the earliest salmon specimens ever collected in North America was a pink taken from British Columbia waters in 1839 by the explorer Sir John Richardson. The skin of this specimen is still on display in the British Museum in London.

Half of all the salmon caught commercially are pink salmon; each year, more than 200 million pinks are taken by commercial fishers.

In the open ocean, pinks swim in vast schools. These schools are often eagerly snapped up by commercial trawlers. Pinks prefer water that is less than 75 feet (23 m) deep, but occasionally, they will range further out to sea; one pink tagged in the Gulf of Alaska south of Anchorage was later caught near Korea, more than 3,500 miles (5,600 km) away. They usually spawn in slow-moving water close to tidal waters, and they are generally attracted to red-colored lures.

Well-known sport-fishing spots for pinks include the Fraser River in British Columbia, and Washington's Puget Sound and Puyallup River.

Sockeye salmon

The runt of the North American salmon family is the sockeye, *Oncorhynchus nerka*. The word *sockeye* comes from the Salish word *suk-kegh*, meaning "fish of fishes." By 1884, the word had been anglicized to *saw-quai*, which was then simplified to its present spelling. Sockeyes are also called reds, redbacks, redfish, red salmon, nerka, bluebacks and Fraser River salmon. Commercial fishers often refer to them as the wonder fish, because of the big bucks they bring in.

Sockeyes are in fact the most important commercial salmon

catch in North America, due to their delicious bright orange, fat-rich flesh. Sockeyes are blue-silver in color, with small speckles on the back, dorsal fin and tail. They have large prominent eyes, with a small pupil taking up about one-third of the total eye diameter.

Spawners are bright red in color, with the males attaining the brightest shades. Spawning females often develop greenish yellow blotches on their sides, and males develop the same shade upon their heads. The spawning female keeps her slim shape, but the male develops a humped back and a sharply hooked nose during spawning time.

Adult sockeyes average 25 inches (63 cm) in length and weigh 3 to 8 pounds (1 to 4 kg). Although undocumented records exist of 15.5-pound (6.9-kg) fish, the largest documented sockeye is a 12.5-pound (5.7-kg) fish taken in the Situk River, Alaska, in 1983. Bright red lures, such as a hook wound with red cotton, are often found to be effective as they mimic shrimp, a favorite sock-eye food.

Kokanees are land-locked sockeyes, fish that never leave their home streams and lakes. They are also called kickininnies, little redfish and little salmon, Kennerly's salmon and silver trout. Coastal Native peoples call them kokos.

Sockeyes can be found from the Sacramento River in California to Point Hope in Alaska, with occasional strays occur-ring along the northern coast of Alaska and as far east as the west coast of Victoria Island, in the Canadian Arctic. They are rare south of the Columbia River.

Asian stocks range from the Kuril Islands off Japan north to the Bering Sea. The major Asian sockeye spawning grounds are on the Kamchatka Peninsula.

In the open ocean, sockeyes stick close to the surface, seldom swimming deeper than 100 feet (33 m). Most of the commercial catch is in water less than 50 feet (15 m) deep.

Of all salmon, sockeyes tend to run the furthest out to sea. Alaska sockeye typically range as far east as 165°E, close to the Kamchatka Peninsula. An Alaskan sockeye tagged in 1972 was caught a year later in Lake Pekulneiskoe on the Russian Federation's Chukotka Peninsula. Another sockeye, tagged in the Wynooche River in Washington, was later caught by a Japanese research ship south of Kiska Island in the Aleutian Islands, about 2,000 miles (3,200 km) away.

Migrating sockeyes often swim in groups, where the swimming is generally easier. Their groups can often be found near shore, in rivers where the currents are weaker. They prefer cold fresh water, and are most comfortable in water that is approximately 56°F (13°C).

The highest numbers of sockeye are found in the Fraser River system in British Columbia (which includes my own beloved Adams River), and the Bristol Bay system in Alaska. The latter system includes Iliamna Lake, the largest salmon-producing lake in the world. The Brooks River in Alaska is famed for its sockeye flyfishing. Other popular sport fishing spots for sockeye include the west coast of Vancouver Island and Lake Washington at Seattle.

Kokanee, the landlocked form of sockeye, prefer water in the 50-to-59°F (10-to-15°C) range that has lots of oxygen. They can be found in lake waters from the surface down to 50 to 60 feet (15 to 18 m), depending on the water temperature. The kokanee was originally native to Oregon, Idaho, Washington, British Columbia and Alaska, but stocking programs have now extended its range to include reservoirs in California, Nevada, Utah, Wyoming and Colorado.

Masu salmon

A seventh salmon species, *Oncorhynchus masu*, the masu or cherry salmon, is found only in Japan and eastern Asia. It may well have been the first Pacific salmon to evolve, as DNA analysis shows it to be the closest biologically to the Atlantic salmon. The Japanese call it *sakura masu*, meaning "cherry trout," for it is found in freshwater streams when the cherry trees are in blossom. There is also a landlocked form of masu known as the *yamame* or *yamabe*. (Some Japanese biologists also recognize an eighth species, *Oncorhynchus rhodurus*, the amago salmon, although most consider the amago a type of masu salmon.)

Masu salmon are renowned for the pink flame markings that appear on the sides of males during the spawning season. The masu generally resemble coho salmon, with shiny silver sides, a blue back, and black spots on the dorsal and tail fins. At spawning time the body color darkens to a dark silver.

Masu average about 9 pounds (4 kg) in weight and 16 to 28 inches (40 to 71 cm) in length. According to the Russian Ministry of Protection of the Environment and Natural Resources, "a record masu salmon of 8.5 kilograms (18.7 pounds) was caught in the Samarga River, Russia, in 1984."[1] The record masu for Japan and Korea are not known.

Masu are found further south than any other wild salmon species, and are common on the Japanese island of Honshu, located at 36°N—the same latitude as Arizona. The highest numbers of masu are found around the Japanese island of Hokkaido. Their range stretches from the Taiko River in Taiwan north to the Primorskaia area in the Russian Federation. Masu are the rarest of all Pacific salmon, with fewer than 100,000 individuals caught each year.

Very little is known about the ocean distribution or adult behavior of this species. The routes taken by masu upon entering the ocean follow no set pattern. Masu seem to prefer the top 60 feet (18 m) of water, rarely going deeper than 100 feet (30 m). Unlike all other salmon, the masu appears to stick very close to shore while at sea. According to Japanese fisheries biologists, no masu have ever been caught east of 145°E longitude, though further investigations may extend this limit.

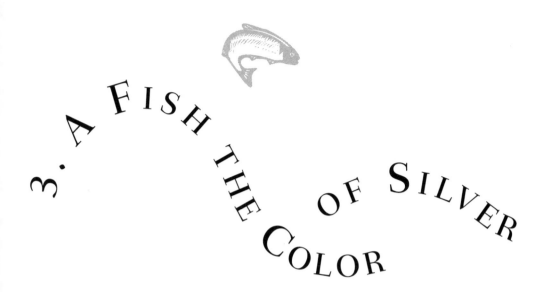

3. A Fish the Color of Silver

"Of all species living in and beside the river, including man, the salmon is... the most beautiful."
BRUCE HUTCHISON, *The Fraser*, 1950

During the research of this book, I visited the public aquariums of Seattle and Vancouver in order to get a "fish-eye" view of my subjects. As I sat in the darkness, watching the ghostly forms gliding through the water like sequined actors on a well-lit stage, it occurred to me just how perfectly the salmon has adapted to its liquid environment. Their bodies are examples of streamlined perfection, their heads coming to a rounded point to reduce friction with water. Water is pushed out of their gills to flow back over their bodies and, in doing so, reduces drag. A thin coating of mucus on the salmon's skin cuts water resistance even further. They are perfect swimming machines.

SWIMMING, BREATHING AND EATING

To many Native tribes the salmon was known simply as "The Swimmer." They swim with a lazy side-to-side motion that is created by the tail and rear half of the body. This motion is powered by a layer of red muscles found just under their skin. To swim, the fish contracts successive muscle segments along one side of its body and bends its tail to that side, then it quickly contracts the

42

muscles along the other side of its body and straightens its tail, pushing it against the water in the process. The push of the tail and body against the water propels the fish forward. The fish's muscles are well supplied with blood vessels and are rich in fat. These muscles fuel the steady swimming. Half of the Pacific salmon's total body weight consists of these muscles alone. In fact, the muscles are strong enough to power 10-foot (3-m) leaps up waterfalls and rapids. These leaps are primarily accomplished by a strong whipping motion of the tail fin. In the midst of these leaps, a salmon can exceed a speed of 14 miles (21 km) per hour.

All salmonids have a number of thin, soft fins. Some are in pairs, like the pectoral fins (located just behind the gill covers) and the pelvic or ventral fins (at the fish's midpoint on its belly). And all salmon have a little triangular fleshy appendage above the pelvic fin that apparently streamlines the fish when the fin is not extended. Other fins stand alone: the dorsal fin, a collapsible sail on the fish's back; the adipose fin, between the dorsal and tail fins; the anal fin, between the ventral and tail fins; and the tail or caudal fin, which brings up the rear.

Each fin serves a specific purpose. The pectoral fins are primarily used for steering. The ventral and dorsal fins keep the fish upright in the water. To hit the brakes, the salmon flares out the pectoral and ventral fins together. The tail fin provides propulsion and is one of the most efficient mechanisms known for forward movement. (The oldest known fossil salmonid tail fin was found near Smithers, British Columbia, and is about 50 million years old; it is almost identical to modern salmonid tail fins.) The dorsal and anal fins help keep the salmon on track as it slices through the water. Both salmon and trout are unique in that they possess an adipose fin. The exact purpose of this fatty little appendage is unknown. Overlapping blocks of muscles called myotomes control the movements of all of the salmon's fins.

As fins are one of the few points on a fish's body that can be easily grabbed by a predator, they are often nibbled or torn off. When this happens, the damaged fin usually regenerates, a handy technique that is being intensively studied by researchers.

Besides fins, fish possess other organs that are absent in humans, notably gills. Anyone who has ever spent time watching a goldfish gulping water in its little glass globe knows that fish breathe by taking in water through their gills. The gills are located behind the mouth cavity, so water taken in through the mouth then passes over the gill filaments. Blood capillaries are close to the surface in the gill filaments so that they can easily take in oxygen from the water, excreting carbon dioxide in the process. The water is then pushed out of the gill covers, which are the flaps that you can see opening and closing behind the fish's eyes.

This process may sound a bit cumbersome, but it is actually quite efficient: gills can extract up to 80 percent of the oxygen from water. Human lungs can remove only about 25 percent of the oxygen from air.

The salmon's heart has four chambers, only two of which are equivalent to the chambers in a human heart. The salmon's blood is the temperature of the surrounding water; a few degrees of warmer water can easily kill a salmon. The heart rate is typically about sixty beats per minute when the fish is snoozing in the shallows, and increases to approximately eighty beats per minute when the fish is roaring through rapids.

Like humans, fish take in food through their mouths. And like some human children, salmon don't chew their food but swallow it whole. A salmon's teeth are used to seize prey. Then they either slice it into bite-sized chunks, or hold it until it can be swallowed whole. The food then slides down the esophagus, a short tube that leads to the stomach. Food is digested in the stomach and then passes in liquid form through the intestine. Undigested food material is egested through the anus, providing food for other creatures and enriching the waters for future generations of salmon. Some waste material is reconstituted by the fish and used to make a crystalline compound called *guanine* that is used in the composition of scales. In many ways, Mother Nature was the first true recycler.

SENSES

Sight

It is a general rule in zoology that predators have eyes located on the front of their heads in order to easily spot their prey. Prey animals, on the other hand, have eyes on the sides of their heads in order to better see all around them. Salmon have eyes that are halfway between a side and frontal position. This denotes their status as both predator and prey.

For the salmon as predator, sight is probably the most important sense. In the retina at the back of the salmon's eye are two types of cells: rods and cones. Cone cells detect color and, in salmon, they are about thirty times more sensitive than rod cells, which detect only tones of gray. A salmon's cone cells are most sensitive to red-orange hues. This explains why red-colored salmon lures seem to be the most effective for anglers. (Fluorescent red is best of all because it keeps its color even in deep water—flat red in deep water often appears black.) This color preference also explains why female spawners find the males' bright red skin so appealing.

Salmon can see all of the full range of colors that humans can see, except they also can see ultraviolet light—giving them a beautiful world indeed. Just think of the range of waters that salmon inhabit: the azure blues of the open sea, the murky browns of the inland rivers, and the crystal-clear of the mountain streams in which they were born. To us it's all just water, but what it looks like to a salmon one can only imagine.

A salmon's eye contains more rod cells than a human eye, and they are more evenly spread over the retina. This allows the salmon to detect tiny movements over a large area, an obvious advantage to any predator. However, salmon are quite nearsighted, rarely seeing more than 3 feet (1 m) in front of them. Even the most attractive artificial fly dangled just out of its sight will probably not be detected.

Salmon eyes lack both lids and lashes, as the flow of water over the eyes performs the same protective functions. In fact, the presence of either a lid or a lash would ruin the perfectly streamlined shape of the fish.

Salmon have monocular vision out of each eye, with a narrow area of binocular vision directly in front, where the two fields of monocular vision overlap. This area of overlap is the preferred hunting zone of salmon as it is the area of best vision.

Above the salmon's head is a cone-shaped area in which it can see clearly. Picture the pointed tip of the cone as lying between the fish's eyes; its flat top lies at the water's surface above the fish's head. The circle of the cone at the water's surface is known as a "Snell circle." The diameter of the top of the cone is just over twice the depth of the fish.

Anglers should note that, although the Pacific salmon has good color sight, artificial flies sitting on the water within the Snell circle will likely appear black against a bright sky, and therefore will not attract the salmon. Flies sitting outside the circle will not be seen clearly at all. It is often the shape of the fly that is most significant to the salmon, not the color.

Directly below the fish is a blind zone that is used to advantage by such salmon predators as mink, otter and larger fish.

Salmon cannot see at all to the rear of their body. Thus, salmon lying quietly in a shallow stream can often be approached from behind and actually caught by hand. I once watched a six-year-old child creep up on a resting sockeye salmon in the Horsefly River of central British Columbia and successfully reach out and grab the fish, to the disgust of a few frustrated adult fishers just downstream.

A salmon's eyes have fixed irises, so there is little control over the amount of light entering the eyes. As a result, bright sun will often send a salmon to deeper depths in order to avoid the light. Thus, midday is often a poor time to go fishing.

Smell

After sight, the most important sense to a salmon is probably smell. In fact, the largest part of the salmon's brain (which is only the size of a peanut) is devoted to smell.

Salmon have an acute sense of smell and can easily detect dissolved substances in concentrations as low as one part per 100 million—the equivalent of half a tablespoon in a large swimming pool. They have two nostrils, called nares, located just in front of their eyes. Each nostril is lined with tiny hairs called cilia, which help to push water back into a minute sac. In each sac there are 500,000 smell receptors per square inch (77,000 per cm^2). If an odor is detected, the smell receptors are responsible for sending chemical messages to the brain.

Unlike human nostrils, a salmon's nares are not used for

breathing. The nares lead only to dead-end sacs, which do not connect with any lung or gill structure.

The salmon's sense of smell is not used much in hunting, but it is the prime sense used during the crucial spawning and migration periods. At these times, chemicals in the water can play havoc with the nares of spawning fish.

Researchers have found that chinook salmon will react quite strongly to tiny amounts of mammalian skin extracts in the water and will actually stop migrating upstream upon smelling this human odor. The chemical responsible for this reaction is an amino acid called L-serine. One has to wonder then if human swimmers in coastal waters or inland lakes have been in any way responsible for keeping salmon from migrating upstream. One also has to wonder what humans smell like to a fish; biologists have found that, to salmon, the smell of bears in the water has the same deterring effect as humans (putting us in stinky company indeed).

Since salmon can detect even extremely small amounts of chemicals in the water, it comes as no surprise that polluted water can completely overwhelm the fish. For example, it has been found that salmon migrating downstream will avoid water in which there is only a tiny trace of copper (2/100 of 1 ppm). Biologists believe that the decline of many salmon stocks in the past can now be attributed to pollutants that entered the water before environmental regulations existed.

The salmon's excellent sense of smell can also be used to advantage. In some areas, biologists concerned with keeping salmon out of the turbines of hydroelectric plants have injected smelly chemicals into the water in order to deter salmon.

Taste

Closely related to smell is taste. Salmon have taste buds in their mouths, on their lips and on their snout—all of which pick up minute chemical messages from the water. Frequently a salmon will take a strange food item into its mouth, give it a quick taste and then spit it out. It is known that salmon can recognize both bitter and sour tastes; their favorite flavors are unknown. The exact tastes preferred by salmon are currently being investigated by researchers searching for more efficient ways of catching dwindling salmon stocks.

Hearing

Since water transmits sounds five times faster than air, underwater sounds can reach salmon very quickly, a significant advantage to any creature that is both predator and prey.

Unlike humans, salmon possess no external ears. External ears would protrude from a fish's body and create drag in the water. This might cause unwanted noise as the fish swam along. Instead, salmon possess an inner ear, and because a salmon's body is about the same density as the surrounding water, sounds pass through to the inner ear unimpaired.

High-frequency vibrations are indirectly detected by tiny bones called otoliths within the inner ear. These vibrations cause the whole fish to vibrate, but since the otoliths are free-floating, they vibrate at a different rate from the rest of the fish. This difference is picked up by sensory hairs (called cilia) that line the inner ear, which then send signals to the fish's brain. The otoliths also serve as balance organs; as they bounce around with a fish's movement, they send information to the sensory cells, reporting on the fish's position relative to perpendicular.

Another hearing mechanism unique to fish is the lateral line. Lying midway along the salmon's flanks are a series of tiny pits lined with even tinier cilia. Sound traveling through the water cause the cilia to vibrate and stimulate attached nerve endings. This line of pits, the lateral line, is most sensitive to low-frequency vibrations, such as those created by gum-booted bozos plodding through a stream. It also can detect pressure changes within the water, giving the fish a good sense of how deep they are in a pond or river. The lateral line also acts as a heat receptor, a warning of rapid changes in water temperature.

Most airborne sounds, such as human voices, cannot be heard by salmon at all. The age-old taboo against talking while fishing then, is pure myth. (Though it does make a handy excuse when you come home empty-handed.)

We tend to think of the underwater world as a dead, silent place, but in fact it is filled with sounds, many coming from the salmon themselves. Although fish do not carry on long-winded conversations, they do communicate with one another. Years ago, when the U.S. Navy developed a microphone sensitive enough to pick up the noise of submerged submarines, they were surprised to hear sounds that were later revealed to be an incredible range of fish sounds. According to Leonard P. Schultz, former Curator of Fish at the Smithsonian Institution, fish may "squeak, toot, grunt, and make musical whistling noises." Pacific salmon are no exception.

It has been found that courting pairs of salmon are especially vocal, and that most of this vocal communicating occurs at night. Exactly what these fishy friends are saying to each other, however, is still unknown.

Each species emits a diagnostic sound. Chinook smolts produce a high-pitched chirpy sound. Adults make a lower knocking noise. Steelheads emit a rapid clucking sound that lasts only for a millisecond.

Just how salmon make these sounds is still not completely understood, but by grinding their teeth, moving muscles that vibrate their air bladders, or rubbing their mouth bones, salmon and other fish can emit a bizarre symphony of underwater sounds.

Of the enormous range of fish sounds produced, only a few can be picked up by salmon. Compared to other fish, a salmon's hearing range is quite restricted.

By determining the exact frequencies heard by the various salmon species, biologists can use sound to either attract or repel them. For example, underwater sounds have been used to deter salmon from entering pumping stations that divert water for agriculture in California's Sacramento River. In this case juvenile chinook salmon traveling downstream come to a fork in the river: the left fork leads to the pumping stations and the right fork leads to the ocean. Speakers suspended from buoys along the entrance to the left fork broadcast sounds in the 50-to-500-Hertz range, a frequency that seems to be the salmon's equivalent of fingernails scraping across a blackboard. Over 65 percent of the fish veer away from these sounds and enter the right fork of the river. The system, developed by the Energy Engineering Services Company of Fort Lauderdale, Florida, has been in place since 1994 and has saved the lives of thousands of salmon.

As every fisher knows, salmon possess a well-developed sense of touch. Nerve receptors embedded in their skin allow them to feel even the slightest touch: a light tickle from an unfriendly finger produces a slight shivering sensation; a harder poke will send the fish on its way. This sense is particularly important during the spawning period, when, for instance, the male and female initiate reproduction by swimming closely together but it also plays an important role in day-to-day life. Imagine gliding through underwater forests of kelp and seaweed, or sliding around rocks oily with growths of algae and moss—in many ways, the salmon's underwater world may be equally as sensuous as our own.

DISEASES AND PARASITES

Despite the carefree appearance of many wild animals, life in the wild is never easy. In both fresh and salt water, salmon are susceptible to a wide variety of bacterial, viral and parasitic infestations. One recent study listed sixty-eight different nasty little beasts lurking in the water, each of which has the ability to infect wild Pacific salmon. Part of what protects the salmon from such infestations is their slimy coat of mucus, which repels bacteria and also makes it difficult for these hitchhikers to attach themselves to the salmon's body.

The largest number of salmon parasites live in fresh water. Since sockeye salmon spend a long period of time in fresh water, they appear to be the most prone of all the salmon species to a wide variety of parasitic infestations. Biologists have identified thirty-six types of parasites that can infest sockeye. In some studies, up to one-third of sockeye fry have been found to host the tapeworm known to biologists as *Eubothrium*. (If you are worried about using sockeye raw in sushi, or marinated, freeze it for four to five hours first to kill any parasites. But most salmon are frozen shortly after being caught anyway.) Young sockeye are also very susceptible to viral infections.

In fresh water, flukes, leech-like critters that attach themselves to a salmon's gills, can seriously reduce the ability of the salmon to breathe properly. Gill infestations of freshwater larval molluscs are also quite common. Gills are also the site for

A Fish the Color of Silver

infestations of a tiny crab-like crustacean known as *Salmincola salmonea*, and a microscopic protozoan called *Dermocystidium*. These tiny little terrors are responsible for the deaths of one-quarter of the adult chinook salmon population spawning at Priest Rapids, Washington, in 1965.

Other microscopic protozoa such as the *Trichodina* may also be a threat, though they seldom cause salmon any serious harm. One exception is the protozoan that causes blister disease (also known as salmon pox), often seen on fall-caught coho.

Bacterial lung disease, a common problem in hatchery salmon, can be transmitted to wild fish. A bacteria called *Chondrococcus* has been responsible for much of the natural decline in salmon in the Columbia River in Washington.

In 1994 and 1995, sockeye in British Columbia's Babine Lake and River system died by the hundreds due to "white spot," or Aich disease. This disease is caused by a tiny organism that flourishes during spells of low water levels and high water temperatures. Biologists are now artificially cooling the water in streams crucial to sockeye in the Babine system in order to control the disease.

The salmon's life at sea isn't any easier. One study of chum salmon found that, while in the open ocean, they could be infested with up to thirty different species of parasites. Sea lice, one of these parasites that lives off salmon blood, are commonly observed clinging to the skin of virtually every species of salmon. These little lobster-like creatures rarely survive once the fish re-enters fresh water, though it is not entirely uncommon for coastal anglers to find them clinging tenaciously to their catch. Occasionally sea lice infestations can be so heavy they affect the fish's ability to swim. The erratic swimming that occurs as a result of this infestation can then often attract predators. The sea lice then can indirectly cause the death of the fish. Most parasites will not cause the death of the host fish, though their presence may affect the fish's overall health and rate of growth. Once a fish reaches the spawning stage, however, fungi that feed upon the very flesh of the fish may appear. Spawning fish are often coated with a white furry fungus known as *Saprolegnia* that can ultimately kill the fish. I once found a spawning female in Cariboo Lake in central British Columbia with fungus completely covering her eyes and snout. The poor fish was swimming in circles, desperately trying to find the outlet at the end of the lake. I netted her and released her there myself, wishing her luck and life.

One of the newer diseases affecting salmon is something called Whirling Disease, a parasitic infection recently discovered in Idaho. The disease was brought to North America during the 1950s in a shipment of infected brown trout eggs. The disease then rapidly spread throughout the United States, and currently it is suspected as one of the major causes of trout declines in Montana.

Whirling Disease is caused by a microscopic protozoan that operates by basically short-circuiting a fish's nervous system. The disease gained its name from the whirling motion of infected fish (they can be seen chasing their tails when frightened). In severe cases, the spine of the fish becomes deformed as a result of its whirling, and this then affects the fish's ability to feed and escape predators. The disease then spreads to other fish when the host fish dies, and the protozoan is carried through the water on spores. Worms then eat the spores, fish eat the worms, and the cycle continues to repeat itself.

There is no known treatment for wild fish infected with Whirling Disease. For the already threatened salmon stocks of Idaho, Whirling Disease may well prove to be last disaster to lead the stocks down the one-way road to extinction.

Even though parasites are generally labeled as threatening little beasts, biologists have occasionally found them to be a useful tool. For example, there is an intestinal worm found only in sockeyes from the Kamchatka Peninsula known as *Truttaedacnitis truttae* (the Latin name is longer than the worm itself), that researchers have used as a kind of ID tag to trace the travels of salmon as they traverse the open ocean.

Longevity

For all their beauty and magic, salmon are short-lived creatures. To find out a salmon's age, biologists use two methods: overall length of the fish and scale ring counts.

The fork length, the length from the front of the head to the fork of the tail fin, is a good rough guide to a fish's age. However, since growth varies from place to place and from species to species, this method requires a great deal of local data in order for accurate length-age tables to be established. In northern Washington, for example, chinook salmon with a fork length of 9 inches (23 cm) are about one year old, while those 30 inches (76 cm) long are about four years old.

A far more accurate technique is that of counting the rings on a fish's scales, the same idea as counting the rings on the trunk of a tree. As salmon grow, tiny rings, known as circuli or sclerites, are laid down upon the scales. The rings of salmon scales consist of narrow winter bands and broader summer bands. These bands record the fast growth of the fish in summer and the slower growth in the winter. Unlike trees, whose rings take years to appear, salmon scales typically develop far more quickly—one or two rings per month rather than a tree's one per year.

The resulting scale patterns are similar to human fingerprints and are used in much the same way. For species like the sockeye, biologists can analyze scale patterns to determine the area in which the fish was reared. Each area tends to produce a distinct pattern of bands that relate to food availability and growth rate. Sockeye from Alaska's Bristol Bay, for example, have relatively few circuli in the first ocean-growth zone. Their summer circuli are generally broad and regular.

By counting the circuli, biologists can ascertain just how long a fish has lived. Pink salmon generally live up to two years, coho two to four years, chum three to five years, steelhead one to five years, and sockeyes four to five years. Masu salmon in Asia may reach five to six years of age. Chinook are the old fogies of the salmon world, living five to eight years—if they can manage to avoid the numerous hazards, both natural and man-made, that they encounter during their fascinating life cycle.

4. THE SALMON LIFE CYCLE: BORN TO DIE

"What is most peculiar is that each salmon searches the stream to the place where he was born."
PEDER CLAUSSØN FRIIS, 1599

For three years, I lived on a remote acreage at the north end of a remote mountain lake. There was no electricity, no phone, and no neighbor for 5 miles (8 km). The compensation was the wildlife: bears regularly strolled across my yard, eagles perched upon my trees, and otters loped along my beach. Just below the end of the lake was a 15-foot (5-m)-high waterfall, where each August I would watch hundreds of salmon perform incredible leaps in order to reach their spawning grounds upstream.

Below the falls was a large basin about 100 feet (30 m) across, filled with quiet pools, glistening rocks, and a number of huge logs that floated round and round in a hypnotic spiral ballet. In many of the pools lay large salmon, their mouths gaping, resting from unsuccessful attempts to scale the falls. They would leap, then rest, then leap again and again. It was tiring just watching them.

Every few minutes a flash of silver would announce another attempt, each leap accompanied by a frantic whipping of the tail, as the salmon tried to literally swim up the falls through the froth and foam. Most failed, only to fall back into the roaring water and be swept downstream into the basin. I wanted so much to help them, to reward them for their efforts, but there was nothing I could do. Along one huge boulder was an old fish ladder, but it lay in disrepair, the victim of financial cutbacks in the federal Department of Fisheries and Oceans. For the sake of a few hundred dollars, hundreds of salmon would die.

Floating in the shallows lay a number of dead salmon, having tragically ended their lives only a short swim from the spot where they were born. Each night their numbers would swell. The fish that fell back into the basin would rest and repeatedly attack the falls until either they made it or they died. Two or three bald eagles would usually park themselves in the nearby treetops, waiting for their next meal to float belly-up onto the rocks. And each morning, size-eleven tracks in the mud revealed to me that black bears had joined the eagles the night before at the salmon buffet.

Almost every day, one or two fishers could be found just below the falls, in flagrant violation not only of the law, but also of the posted notices that lined the river's banks. Many of these fishers would later tell me that they "weren't catching as many salmon here as they used to," without ever clueing in that they might be part of the problem. Very few salmon make it through a complete life cycle to mature and spawn; the removal of even a few dozen fish can spell disaster to small salmon runs such as this one.

In the early 1900s, stories of the bizarre salmon life cycle were dismissed as utter nonsense. In 1925, one book on fish declared bluntly: "It is the prevailing impression that the salmon have some special instinct which leads them to return to spawn on the same spawning grounds where they were originally hatched...we do not believe it to be true." But not only is it true but it is steeped in tragedy.

Born in freshwater streams, salmon migrate to the ocean, reach adulthood, and then make a dash back to the waters of their birth, overcoming incredible obstacles along the way in order to do so. Their will to survive is mind-numbing.

At the spawning grounds, they lay their eggs, gasp their last breaths and finally die. It is a life cycle more touching and more tragic than any of the other myriad miracles in the animal kingdom. And, as it does with most animals, it all begins with a tiny egg.

THE EGG

We've all seen salmon eggs—reddish-orange, translucent, and about a quarter-inch (6 mm) in diameter—looking all the world like smaller versions of the horrible cod-liver-oil pills my mother used to make me swallow years ago. But what most people have not seen is the tremendous number of eggs laid by a female salmon. A single spawning female in the fall can lay up to 20,000 eggs at one time, of which 85 to 90 percent will die before hatching.

Some of these drops of life will freeze during unusually cold winters. Some will die from heat during periods of drought. Others will wash away during flash floods in the spring.

For the first four weeks after fertilization, salmon eggs are incredibly susceptible to physical shock. In hatcheries, they are never handled during this period. In the wild, many are crushed by cattle and logging equipment moving through streams, and many are gobbled up by fish, mink, otters, birds and leeches.

But some do survive. About a week after fertilization, an embryo can be seen moving within the egg. About three weeks later, the most visible feature of the embryo are two huge black eyes (at this stage they are termed to be in the "eyed stage").

Gradually a yellow yolk sac laced with blood vessels develops. The sac is a kind of built-in feed bag, containing proteins, fats and salts that feed the embryo for many months, generally October through May. The embryo develops on top of the egg, curled around the yolk sac like an attentive mother protecting her young. I once held a handful of eyed eggs at a hatchery and stared wondrously through their amber walls. Perhaps these very eggs would grow to be the few—the very few—adult salmon that would successfully complete the journey back home years later. I carefully set them back in the water, where they lay glittering like precious gems.

The time of hatching partly depends on water temperature. Tests on steelhead eggs showed that eggs kept in 60°F (16°C) water took 18 days to hatch; those in 38°F (3°C) water took 101

The Salmon Life Cycle: Born to Die

days. But water that is too warm spells disaster: chinook eggs will suffer a 50 percent mortality if the water temperature exceeds 61°F (16°C). Often it is the eggs at the bottom of a nest that hatch first, due to the slight warming effect created by the eggs and rocks above.

In order to hatch, the tadpole-shaped embryo secretes an enzyme that eats through the wall of the egg. The embryo then twists around within its egg, jerking frantically until the wall breaks. The exact time of hatching is triggered by the oxygen level within the egg. When the oxygen requirements of the embryo exceed the oxygen-absorbing capability of the egg wall, enzyme production increases and hatching occurs. In hatcheries, humans can artificially trigger hatching by lowering the oxygen level of the water.

Some embryos never hatch and some only partially hatch—they manage to push their heads through the egg wall, but lack the strength to pull their bodies through as well. All such weaklings are doomed to die. The tiny larva that do successfully emerge are called alevins.

THE ALEVIN

The alevin is an alien-looking creature with big black eyes and a large yellow yolk sac. The large eyes make the alevin very sensitive to light, but may help detect predators. In order to avoid bright light levels, alevins flee into weeds or bottom gravels. In one experiment, fifty sockeye alevins starved to death in a brightly lit aquarium tank rather than emerge into the light and feed.

Water temperature, the oxygen levels, and the amount of nutrients found in the water determine the growth rate of alevins. For most salmon species, the alevin growth rate doubles between 32°F (0°C) and 41°F (5°C), and doubles again at 50°F (10°C). The alevin absorb oxygen through a thick vein that runs through their yolk sacs.

Alevins live in stream bottom gravels for three to four months until their yolk sacs, their source of nourishment, are used up. Most alevins wait until night to sneak out of the protective gravels. Some will emerge with lots of yolk left, an apparent survival mechanism in waters where there is insufficient food to sustain them.

When the alevin has completely eaten up its yolk sac, it becomes a free-swimming tiny fish called a fry. Many of the "minnows" caught by children throughout the Pacific Northwest are actually salmon fry.

THE FRY

It is in the fry stage that the juvenile salmon finally begin to dress like adults, with dark backs and light bellies. Chum fry develop a distinctive blue-green iridescence. Most species of fry develop vertical bars on their sides known as parr marks, a term originally applied only to Atlantic salmon. Parr marks are very effective in camouflaging fry hiding in weed beds. Chinook fry have the most parr marks. Pink salmon fry have no parr marks.

To begin swimming, fry must first be able to float. To do this, they inflate their air bladders, balloon-like organs located deep within their bodies. These organs may have served ancient fishes as lungs at one time, allowing them to survive when droughts left them high and dry. The modern lungfish can survive for a year out of water wrapped in a ball of mud, living only upon the air trapped inside its lungs.

To inflate its air bladder, a salmon fry will swim up to the surface of the stream head first, like a tiny silver dart, and gulp in mouthfuls of air. Several trips to the surface may be needed in order to completely inflate the air bladder so that the fry will attain neutral buoyancy. Once the fry attains neutral buoyancy it will begin to swim, feed and explore its watery world. Sometimes silt or debris can block the fry's vertical route. In that case the fry will follow tiny cracks and underground streams in a horizontal direction until it finds open water. Fry can thus miraculously appear in ditches or wells some distance from the stream gravels, sparking many believe-it-or-not tales among rural housewives.

The salmon's swim bladder is rather unusual in that it lies below the fish's center of gravity. This lower center of buoyancy tends to roll the fish up sideways, which may seem awkward but is actually advantageous, giving them the ability to turn quickly. When a salmon chases a prey fish to the surface, it can then arch its body sideways by rolling 90 degrees onto its side just as it reaches the water's surface; in this way it can then quickly turn and zip back down to the depths and safety. The low center of buoyancy makes this difficult maneuver easier, and hence enhances the fish's chances of catching its prey. Less active feeders, like perch, have a center of buoyancy above the center of gravity, making them less agile. Freshwater fish that feed on the bottom of lakes and other water systems don't even have swim bladders.

To the angling layman, a salmon zipping to the surface to feed and then rolling sideways to dive may appear to be a fish feeding upon the surface. The tendency of the angler would then be to use a top-water fly or lure, a waste really, since the salmon is actually feeding below the surface. Anglers who use top-water flies when they see the swirl of the salmon's tail on the surface are guaranteed to go home empty-handed—a hard and frustrating lesson.

Salmon fry are opportunistic feeders, dining on whatever happens to be available. Chinook fry are the wolves of the salmon family; they tend to stay in one spot in a strong current and snatch up just about any organic matter that drifts by, be it dead or alive. Most other salmon fry feed on bottom-dwelling animals and microscopic plankton, switching to tiny insects, and then to small fish, as they grow larger. To sustain normal growth, fry require 50 percent protein in their diet. One of the richest sources of protein to salmon fry is plankton.

Technically the word *plankton* means any living thing that moves by drifting or floating on top of the water. Colloquially it is often also used as slang for floating microscopic organisms. If the organism is a plant, it is called "phytoplankton"; if it is animal, it is called "zooplankton."

Seventy percent of all zooplankton are tiny crustaceans. Many plankton have bizarre shapes: some look like vases, some like little golf balls, and others like little lobsters distorted by wavy funhouse mirrors.

Many planktonic organisms are incredibly tiny; they could easily fit into the period at the end of this sentence. The relationship between salmon and plankton is a complex one, and some biologists now believe that the boom-and-bust cycles of salmon runs may be directly related to fluctuations in the water's plankton levels.

As fry grow, their food habits often follow whatever Mother Nature serves up each season. One study of sockeye fry in British Columbia found them munching on the tiny crustacean *Diaptomus* in the spring, on chironomids (gnat-like insects) in the summer, and back to another crustacean, *Daphnia*, in the fall. Many areas in the western United States have an orderly appearance of midges, chironomids and mayflies in May; damselflies and caddisflies in June; dragonflies in July/August; and water boatmen and backswimmers in September/October.

One of the key elements to successful salmon fly fishing is the ability to choose the correct insect-imitation fly for the proper time of year—in fishing jargon, to "match the hatch." A few questions directed to the local fish and game warden or to the local sporting-goods shop are often well worth the while of eager fly fishers because who would be more likely to know what kind of insect the fish are feeding off at that time of season? (I once asked a grizzled old fly fisher plying one of Washington's famed streams what he was using. He stared at me for a second, narrowed his eyes, and declared solemnly: "Prayer, my son. Lots of prayer.")

Of all insects, the two most important salmon food items are mayflies and caddisflies. As a quick rule of thumb, mayflies have short antenna and are transparent with lacy wings, while caddisflies are fuzzy beasts with long antenna and mottled cream and black wings.

The word "mayfly" is a general term for more than 2,000 species of insects. Mayfly larvae, or nymphs, that are hatched in rivers and streams, have six legs and a two- or three-pronged tail. Around May, after about a year in its nymphal stage, the mayfly floats to the surface of the stream and molts, emerging with beautiful long wings. As the wings dry, the defenseless mayfly becomes a sitting duck for hungry salmon. Shortly after the first molt, the mayfly undergoes a second molt into an even larger insect. Mayflies are the only insects that will molt again after their wings have become functional. Clouds of mayflies form above streams as the males search for the females; young salmon will often leap out of the water to feed on this aerial buffet.

There are more than 7,000 species of caddisflies, all of which are moth-like with hairy wings. Caddisfly larvae can be distinguished by their habit of building protective houses around themselves from tiny bits of sand and debris glued together with a silky gooey substance secreted by the larvae itself. After about a year the larvae mature in these protective houses into fly-shaped adults. Salmon will feed on both the larvae and the adults, but avoid the tasteless houses.

Typically, salmon fry will rise to near surface at dawn or dusk in order to feed, although daytime hatches of tiny invertebrates are rarely passed up. Fry cannot feed in total darkness, since they require sunlight in order to see their food. Insects unfortunate enough to fall upon the surface of a salmon stream or lake are favorite fare for many species. The larval stages of midges, which hide around wet rocks and plants, also play an important role in the diet of young fry.

From May to July, the fry's intake of food may increase tenfold. After gorging on mayflies and caddisflies, fry grow to a length of 3 to 6 inches (6 to 15 cm), at which point they are known as fingerlings, though there is no exact length in which a fry becomes a fingerling.

Lab tests have shown that salmon fry are capable of surviving without food for a couple of days without dire consequences. In fact, fry have been known to survive many weeks of starvation.

In many rivers and lakes, a number of other small fish compete for the same food items as young salmon. Juvenile sticklebacks and whitefish, for example, in sufficient numbers may even force salmon to leave by taking over a feeding area.

Salmon fry and fingerlings are themselves a favorite food for many predators, including trout, char, squawfish, suckers, and even older salmon. In the Naknek Lake system in Alaska, lake trout numbers increase dramatically when sockeye fry migrate between lakes. A year after a major sockeye run in British Columbia's Adams River, the trout population in adjacent Shuswap Lake usually explodes due to the abundant food supply. Since the damming of the Columbia River, squawfish have increased tremendously, killing thousands of salmon fingerlings annually.

Char also regularly gorge on young salmon; a Dolly Varden char was once opened up to reveal ninety sockeye fry in its stomach. In

1971, arctic char in the Wood River Lake system in Alaska devoured an incredible 3 million salmon fry, almost two-thirds of the total lake population. Mergansers, gulls, loons, herons, mink, otter and raccoons also enjoy a salmon supper.

Fry generally use one of two techniques to evade their predators: panic and hiding. The panic response sets fry darting off in all directions, confusing the predator and making it difficult to single out a target. Hiding has fry literally secreting themselves among weeds or the tight crevices of bottom rocks that are too small to allow larger predators to pursue them.

Pink salmon fry seem to be most vulnerable to surface predators, due to their habit of brainlessly zipping around near the surface when attacked, rather than diving to the protection of deeper water.

In one ten-year study of pink salmon, up to 86 percent of fry were killed annually by other fish. In fact, only about 10 to 30 percent of all salmon fry ever make it to the next stage of their lives.

It is at the three- or four-month-old stage in the salmon life cycle that things begin to get complicated. Some fry stay where they are and others will move to nearby lakes. Some move downstream and some upstream. Some immediately migrate toward the sea.

Most chinook fry stay in large rivers for at least three months to a year. (Some biologists divide chinook into two types: stream types, which spend one or more years in fresh water; and ocean types, which migrate to the sea during their first year.)

Most sockeye and coho fry immediately head for lakes, where they will then stay for one to three years, although some sockeye fry spend up to a year in marshes or sloughs.

Masu salmon fry spend at least one year in river systems.

Steelhead fry normally live for one or two years in fresh water before traveling to the sea. Their time in fresh water seems to be directly related to temperature: the colder the water, the longer the stay. California steelhead tend to go to sea after only a year in fresh water. Oregon steelhead stay for two years, and British Columbia steelhead usually wait for three years.

Most chum fry head seaward immediately, but some spend weeks or months in freshwater streams.

Almost all pinks migrate directly to the sea. Some pinks even skip the freshwater stage completely and spawn in brackish intertidal areas.

Mature fingerlings that survive the onslaught of predators and are ready to travel to the sea are called smolts.

THE SMOLT

When fry reach the smolt stage, their color changes from a dull, barred scheme to the familiar shiny silver of the adult salmon. The shiny coat may look garish to human eyes, but in the sun-slashed upper waters of the Pacific, it provides perfect camouflage. (The different appearances of fry, smolts and spawners led early biologists to class them as separate species.)

The change in color, the first step in smolt migration, is apparently triggered by thyroid gland activity, which in turn is triggered by the increasing length of the day. This is indirectly measured by the pineal gland, located at the top of the fish's head above the brain, which increases its activity upon prolonged exposure to light.

In juvenile salmon, the skin and skull over the top of the pineal gland are thin and translucent, allowing light to enter. As the fish mature, the skin and skull thicken and become opaque; to many biologists this suggests that the pineal gland is not as significant to adult fish.

Some researchers believe that water temperature is a significant factor in smolt migration. It has been suggested that spring water temperatures above 40°F (4°C) are a sign to fish to start migrating. In many areas, sockeye smolts begin to migrate within days of ice breakup.

Thus there is a complex interrelationship of factors that control smolt migration. During extra-long winters, for example, stream water remains cold and prevents smolts from migrating. These smolts will then change back to the dull appearance of fry. A year later, they will once again change into their suit of shiny armor and try to march off to sea.

Most smolts migrate in the spring. They often prefer to move under cover of the night, with many runs peaking around midnight and dwindling as dawn approaches. In Alaska, millions of sockeye smolts from Lake Iliamna were once observed migrating downstream; most migrated between 10 p.m. and 2 a.m. Often there is a second run just before dawn. The sight of thousands of silvery smolts is a jaw-dropping sight, with clouds of fish strung like stars across the breadth of the stream. Migration usually stops in the summer, when the surface waters become too warm.

As they move downstream, smolts will swim and also lazily let themselves drift with the current. In turbulent water, they have been known to turn themselves and go downstream tail first in order to protect their heads from the strong currents, like humans turning their back in windstorms.

As the smolts trek seaward, biological changes occur in their bodies which allow them to live in salt water. In fresh water, the salt concentration within salmon is higher than in the surrounding water, so through the process of osmosis (the tendency of fluids to pass through semi-permeable membranes from areas of low concentration to high concentrations, thus creating equal concentrations on both sides of the membrane), fresh water is forced into the fish.

In salt water, the opposite occurs: water flows out from the fish into the sea. To prevent drying out, salmon must drink salt water in order to maintain the proper salt concentration within their bodies. The amount of water ingested sometimes amounts to a third of the fish's body weight each day. Chloride-secreting cells also develop within the salmon's body to aid in salt production. Most salmon species need to maintain a salt level of 0.075 percent in their body fluids, whereas the ocean is 3 to 4 percent salt. If a salmon produces or ingests too much salt, the excess is excreted through the gills. The process of adjusting to salt water for the first time doesn't happen overnight; in chinooks, it takes at least 200 hours (this number varies between subspecies).

Often smolts will stay in inshore estuaries for periods that range from two days to three months, during which time they adapt to the salt water and fatten up before heading for the open ocean. The upper water layer in estuaries is rich in plankton, and both insects and crustaceans add variety to the smolts' diet. During this time the smolts can eat so much that they often double or triple in weight.

The Salmon Life Cycle: Born to Die

64

Unfortunately for the salmon, other animals feed in estuaries as well, and gatherings of smolts can provide a rich buffet for hordes of predators including gulls, terns, herons and larger fish. Most smolts found in estuaries are only 3 to 4 inches (7 to 10 cm) long. There is some evidence that larger smolts are better able to evade predators.

When the smolts do leave the estuaries, most will head north, carefully sticking to within approximately 25 miles (40 km) of the coast. Most stay over the continental shelf, concentrating near the shelf break, where currents bring in food from deeper water.

Most juvenile salmon start out by feeding near shore, gobbling up the thick plankton blooms that Mother Nature thoughtfully provides each spring. They then swim in a large counter-clockwise loop north to Alaska, west along the Aleutians, and then south to the open ocean, covering more than 3,000 miles (4,800 km). Swimming speeds range from 3 to 16 miles (5 to 26 km) per day. The route is boosted by the strong Alaska Current, which flows north into Alaska, and the Alaska Stream, which flows west toward the Aleutians. These currents move at up to ten times the swimming speed of juvenile salmon and help the young fish to conserve energy.

Some salmon do not follow this pattern at all. Columbia River smolts, for example, head south as they hit salt water and ride the California Current to the waters off Oregon and California. Hatchery fish from British Columbia also sometimes head south, and have been caught as far south as Coos Bay, Oregon. Why these fish have to buck traditional routes, no one knows.

Other stocks of coho and chinooks spend extended periods inshore along the British Columbia coast or in the protected rich waters of Puget Sound in Washington. These stay-at-homes never reach the size of their oceangoing cousins, but constitute an important part of the sport fishery. In all of these areas, the ocean is where the young salmon feed and grow to adulthood.

The first few months of ocean life are dangerous ones for smolts. At this point in their lives, the young fish have no experience evading the big bullies that lurk in the open ocean. Even other salmon take their toll; mature coho salmon often prey on pink and chum smolts in estuaries and just offshore. One study of chum salmon found that 31 to 46 percent were killed by predators

Early morning in the Adams River valley, one of the most famous salmon spawning grounds in North America.

This chinook salmon from the Fraser River can be distinguished from other salmon species by its spotted lower tail fin lobes and dark colored lower gums.

A steelhead salmon in its freshwater garb.

A male pink salmon, also commonly referred to as a humpback, from the Fraser River, displays the prominent hump on its back.

A sockeye salmon, commonly considered the runt of the North American salmon family, from the Fraser River, British Columbia.

Sockeye salmon turn bright red at spawning time.

A chum salmon scales a small waterfall near Hyder, Alaska in an effort to reach its spawning ground.

A coho salmon looks very similar to a chinook except for spots on the upper lobes of its tail fins and light-colored lower gums.

During migration salmon are forced to hurdle natural obstacles such as this beaver dam in order to reach their spawning grounds.

A pair of gaping sockeye in mid-spawn signal the end of the spawning ritual.

A dead salmon covered with the furry white Saprolegnia fungus.

The Chilliwack River in British Columbia is filled with migrating cohoes in early summer.

Fisheries biologists tagging fish in an effort to learn more about salmon migration patterns.

Fishermen trying their luck at dawn in the Campbell River.

in their first four days at sea. In a study of sockeye spawning in Babine Lake, British Columbia, about 90 percent of ocean mortality occurred during the first four months.

LIFE AT SEA

Relatively little is known about the life of salmon once they reach the ocean. The rough open seas are a difficult spot to conduct field research. Marine biologist William G. Pearcy was quite accurate when he wrote, "The marine ecosystem has been neglected as an unfathomable 'black box,' into which young salmonids disappear and from which, if all goes right, adults emerge."[1] It is often the case (sadly) that the only time salmon are observed at sea is when they are on the end of a fishing line.

A salmon in its first summer at sea is called a "grilse." Males that become sexually mature after one year at sea are called "jacks." Jacks are particularly aggressive on the line, and are therefore eagerly sought after by sport fishers (occasionally a female salmon will also mature at one year; these fish are predictably known as "jills").

The movements of salmon at sea are varied, and relate to a variety of factors, including food availability, sea-bottom geography and climatic patterns.

Climatic patterns can help determine which salmon species will be found in a certain area. Generally speaking, sockeye and chum prefer waters where the sea-surface temperatures are quite cold. Coho and chinook seem to prefer warmer waters. It is now known that the southern limit of salmon distribution at sea is determined primarily by sea-surface temperature.

It is also known that there is a general pattern that sees salmon heading to the southern parts of their ocean range during the winter and the northern part of their ocean range in the spring, very much like seagoing swallows. Biologists believe that, during very cold winters, salmon will move south and become concentrated, though this makes them easy prey for predators such as the northern fur seal. During warm winters, salmon generally disperse over large areas of the northern Pacific Ocean, where they are less susceptible to predators. Thus, the overall survival rates of salmon can be affected by weather patterns.

It has also been found that the warm ocean temperatures of the 1980s may have had a beneficial effect on salmon in the Gulf of Alaska. There appears to be a direct relationship between growth rate and sea-surface temperatures.

Sea-bottom geography plays a role in concentrating schools of salmon over shallow areas where abundant food can be obtained. Reefs, rockpiles and points of land are all popular salmon lunch spots for both lone fish and large schools.

Many salmon tend to run at sea in schools, and within these schools it has been suggested that a fish's version of pecking order may exist. It has been found, for example, that socially dominant chum tend to have strong vertical markings, while subordinate chum have predominantly horizontal patterns.

There may also be a rough social ranking according to size, where the largest salmon will rush in to grab the choice food morsels. Larger salmon also tend to be more successful at escaping predators.

As a general rule, the largest salmon are found in the northern half of their range at sea. This fulfills Bergmann's Rule, which states that, for most species, body size will increase from south to north. The core of this rule of thumb is heat efficiency; larger bodies tend to be more efficient at conserving heat, all other things being equal. There are even data to support this: all record sized salmon of the six North American species have been caught north of 48°N latitude, in either Alaskan or British Columbian waters.

Of all the possible factors, food availability determines many of the salmon's movements at sea for the simple reason that much of the salmon's time at sea is devoted to eating.

Eating habits

Sockeye, pink, and chum salmon primarily eat oceangoing plankton and crustaceans such as shrimp. Shrimp-like *Euphausia*, commonly known as krill, are an especially popular sockeye food item. Krill are so common in the open ocean that some biologists believe they may someday be regularly harvested for human consumption. By the year 2000, you may well be dining on "McKrill" burgers.

Pink salmon have very soft mouths and almost exclusively feed on tiny plankton. The main plankton in the open ocean are copepods, tiny crustaceans whose jerky swimming movements attract many predators.

Plankton avoid light, rising to the surface at night, and sinking to greater depths during the day. Salmon often follow the same pattern, rising to the surface at night to gorge upon the plankton.

Research on sockeyes, the most intensely studied of all salmon, show that they may travel between 10 and 50 miles (16 and 80 km) per day in search of plankton swarms. An average day will find them swimming for up to seventeen hours and resting or eating for the remaining seven. They may put on 95 percent of their total body weight during their years at sea. Sockeyes also tend to travel the furthest out to sea; chinooks and cohos tend to travel the least distance. As they mature, sockeyes switch to squid as a favorite food item.

The oceanic feeding habits of steelhead have not been well documented. Commercial catches of steelhead at sea are often incidental to the main target—chinook, coho and sockeye—and are often discarded, wasting a precious opportunity for biologists to gather valuable information.

Chinooks and cohos start out dining on plankton and crustaceans, but then switch as they grow to small fish such as herring, mackerel, pilchard, sand lance and candlefish, as well as squid and jellyfish.

The herring is probably the most abundant near-surface fish in the Pacific Ocean. As such, it is a prime food source for salmon at sea and a prime bait of commercial salmon fishers. One study of coho foods at sea found that small fish, such as herring, made up 75 percent of the coho's diet. Herring can make up two-thirds of the ocean diet of chinook salmon. When herring are attacked by salmon, they often mass together to form a "herring ball," which makes it difficult for a predatory salmon to choose a single target. These balls are often good indicators that salmon are in the area.

During July and August, coho and chinook force smaller fish inshore. Their sudden appearance is a big clue to salmon fishers to get their nets ready; the feeder fish often try to hide among the kelp beds that line the shore, and so these kelp beds are a good spot to fish for salmon. Other popular salmon feeding spots are areas of high turbulence, such as the passes between islands, where increased oxygen levels attract increased numbers of live foods. Hakai Pass, for example, off British Columbia's west coast, has long been famous for its giant chinooks.

Predation upon salmon

Salmon are prey to a wide variety of ocean predators, including larger fish such as halibut, Pacific lampreys, seals, sea lions, dolphins and whales. There is even a 10-foot (3-m) shark that is commonly called the salmon shark because of its favorite meal. In Alaska, the chubby beluga whales that annually swim up the Kvichak River put on much of their bulk dining on salmon heading out to sea.

One of the most efficient predators of salmon in coastal waters is the beluga's cousin, the killer whale or orca. When chinook salmon start their race back to marine estuaries before spawning, pods of hungry killer whales are often waiting *en route*. If a chinook salmon seeks safety in the crevice of a rock wall, killer whales have been known to push so hard against the rock that the rock will leave a temporary dent in the whale's head. Killer whales have also been known to push their head against the rock face that is hiding the salmon and then suddenly pull away, thus creating a back eddy in the water that will literally suck the fish out of its hiding spot. The orca's intelligence can be humbling.

Another type of fishing technique used by killer whales calls for group cooperation. A group of whales will encircle a school of salmon, splashing their mighty tails on the surface of the water in order to herd the fish into a small, panicked concentration below the water's surface. Once the salmon are trapped below the water's surface, other whales waiting below can then feed. The same technique has been picked up by seine (net) fishers, who encircle a school of salmon with a circular net and then close a string at the bottom in order to trap the fish.

With a diet of over 400 pounds (180 kg) of fish a day, killer whales can devour a lot of salmon. Commercial fishers have known this for years and, before the whales were protected, took every opportunity to kill them. In one study years ago, about one in four of the killer whales captured for the public aquarium business was found to have bullet holes in its body. However, compared with the hundreds of millions of salmon taken by humans each year, the number taken by orcas is really of little consequence.

Some fishers have allied with the whales, using them as guides to lead them directly to the salmon. According to Bob Dick, a Native fisher who plies the waters off the coast of British Columbia, "when the blackfish [killer whales] are coming, more'n likely they're driving schools of scared salmon in front of 'em. So what you do is, you make your set [of nets] directly in their path."[2] Others simply look for the sparkle of scales upon the water to tell them that killer whales are feeding on salmon below.

Although predators are not the main reason for declining salmon stocks, early biologists were often quick to mistakenly pinpoint them as the reason for the declines. In 1915, the Canadian Fisheries Department killed 2,875 sea lions in order to protect the salmon. Between 1931 and 1937, 6,430 sea lions were machine-gunned to death in B.C. coastal waters.

The folly was almost repeated in 1996 when five sea lions in Puget Sound were sentenced to death in an effort to "preserve" a steelhead run. Luckily, this time around wiser minds prevailed.

Resentment against sea mammals that feed upon salmon runs so high among the American commercial fishing fraternity that in 1994 they were able to successfully lobby for an amendment to the Marine Mammal Protection Act to allow for the legal killing of animals known to endanger salmon populations. The first time the amendment was acted upon was in November 1994, when permission was given to kill sea lions feasting on steelhead at the entrance to the fish ladder at Ballard Locks, on the Lake Washington Ship Canal. It was the first time official permission had been granted to kill marine mammals in the United States since the animals had been given legal protection.

The truth is that much of the anger is misdirected. Studies have shown that salmon typically play a very small role in the diet of the Steller sea lion. Canadian biologist David J. Spalding found that all of British Columbia's sea lions and harbor seals together consume only about 2.5 percent of the human annual salmon catch. "Predation at this level," he wrote, "is believed to be of negligible importance in the reduction of existing salmon...stocks."[3]

In fact, for years many sea mammals have been falsely labeled as big-time salmon killers. Continued research, however, is quickly dispelling these old folk tales. Harbor seals, for example, are sometimes shot on sight by commercial fishers, but studies have found that only 4 percent of their diet is made up of salmon. One can only hope that the research will quickly catch up with current fishing practices so that this kind of needless slaughter will stop.

Depending on the species, salmon that evade the many hazards of life at sea spend on to seven years in the ocean before returning to fresh water. Sockeye salmon generally return at three to six years of age. Fraser River sockeye almost exclusively return at the age of four.

Pinks are two-year fish, returning to fresh water after about eighteen months at sea. Their fixed two-year life span means that two different stocks of salmon may use the same stream for spawning, alternating year after year. In most areas, one year has a dominant run of pinks and the following year is poor for pinks. The Fraser River, for example, has a dominant run in odd-numbered years, and the Queen Charlotte Islands has even-year booms of pinks. In years when pinks are few and far between, chum salmon populations soar, apparently filling the same feeding niche. For some reason, there is a strong tendency for odd-year pinks to be larger than even-year fish.

Sometimes a run of pinks does not show up, and this is termed an "off" year. When this occurs, biologists often try to transplant hatchery-bred pinks in order to boost the population.

As for the remaining species of salmon, their return from the ocean runs as follows: Chum salmon head home after three to four years at sea. Coho feed at sea for only sixteen to eighteen months. Steelhead spend at least two years at sea, and the masu salmon of Japan stays at sea for one and a half years.

Chinook stay in the open ocean the longest, often for three to seven years, during which time they can grow to enormous sizes.

During the salmon's time at sea, the various stocks mix freely. There is even an area in the western North Pacific where Asian and North American salmon mix and mingle, although generally Asian stocks predominate west of 175° longitude and North

American stocks are most common east of this line. But once the fish reach sexual maturity and are ready to head back to fresh water, each stock separates.

When salmon reach maturity and head back to the rivers of their birth, they are known as spawners. For most salmon species, 90 to 99 percent of the population never reach the spawning stage due to the many trials of salmon life.

THE SPAWNER

From the sea...

How the salmon manage to return to the rivers of their birth is one of the great mysteries of science and one of the great stories of the wild kingdom. Most of the current knowledge regarding this fish migration has dribbled in over the years through fish tagging.

The tagging of fish is not new; one of the earliest records of tagging comes from Sweden in the fifteenth century, when Frederick II placed rings around the necks of pike to trace their travels. Over the subsequent 400 years, a number of different tagging methods have been developed.

Much of the early tagging of salmon was cruel and thoughtless, often resulting in the untimely death of the fish. The removal of a ventral fin, for example, was a handy technique that made the fish easily recognizable, but was soon found to hamper the fish's ability to swim and thus escape predators. Similarly, medieval measures such as the clipping of dorsal or tail fins, or even the removal of a little piece of the salmon's lower jaw, are now largely a thing of the past.

Today, the use of plastic or metal tags attached to the gill coverings or fins is one of the methods used. Sonic transmitters or magnetized steel wires that are inserted internally, or injected into the fish's snout is another method. Tattoos may be burned or cold-branded into the skin, radioactive isotopes may be injected into the fish, or fluorescent dyes may be sprayed onto the fish's body. Salmon may even be artificially infected with unique parasites so that catches at sea will reveal the fish's origin.

As ingenious as these techniques are, they still often result in dead fish. Salmon are very susceptible to disease if their protective mucus coating is accidentally rubbed off. In addition to this danger, any external mark, tag or abnormality sends up a red flag to predators, and thus marked fish are often gobbled up faster than unmarked fish.

For this latter reason, internal tags are the most commonly used practice for marking today. Most common of all is the magnetized steel wire injected into the fish's nose. This wire can then be detected by the use of strong magnets, and the marked fish is then killed in order to remove the wire. The wire may be color-coded, or a binary code may be noted by putting a series of tiny nicks on the wire. In some cases, the adipose fin—a fin not used in swimming—is removed from chinooks and coho to aid in the identification and collection of wired fish.

Many modern transmitters can be detected electronically by instruments placed strategically at narrow passages heading in or out from the ocean or at fish gates. Some fisheries departments will also pay fishers directly for returned tags, or will use lotteries or draws of returned tags—surely one of the more rewarding times in history that anglers have been paid to fish! However, these tagging programs often reveal more about the movement of boats than about the movement of fish. Critics have also pointed to the high cost of tagging operations compared with the low recovery rate; in many operations, it is not unusual to recover less than 1 percent of the tagged fish.

However, tagging can provide a wealth of information to fish scientists. Multichannel transmitters can provide data on swimming speed, heart rate, gill rate and water conditions. Recaptured fish are weighted and measured, and growth rates can then be determined since the date of tagging. A lack of retrieved tagged fish may be an indirect measure of the high death rate of the fish. But primarily tags are used to trace the travels of salmon in an attempt to unravel the mystery of migration.

To the river...

People have long wondered how it is that salmon can find their way back to their natal streams, first through the vast ocean, and then up freshwater rivers branched with hundreds of side streams.

In ancient times, the migration of animals was well known, and explained through folklore. Aristotle thought that, when Atlantic eels appeared seemingly out of nowhere during their migrations, they had spontaneously grown from the *gas entera*, the entrails of the sea.

Along the Pacific Ocean, ancient peoples were no less intrigued by the migrations of the salmon. The Tlingit and Haida believed that salmon were actually a race of spirits who lived in human form beneath the sea. They thought that once a year these spirits would assume the bodies of salmon and swim up the streams to feed the Native people, who welcomed them with the First Salmon ceremony. In this rite, the first salmon caught migrating upstream was taken by a priest and placed reverently upon an altar. It was treated as an honored guest and was placed with its head pointing upstream, so that the rest of the salmon would continue in that direction.

In more recent times, biologists have discovered a few facts that help answer the riddle of migration. They have found, for example, that salmon fry can maintain a compass direction from the position of the sun, and so may use the sun as a directional aid in the open ocean. The angle of the sun may even tell salmon the latitude, enabling them to find the river mouth that leads to the stream where they were born.

Recent experiments have confirmed that salmon in laboratory tanks change orientation when overhead lights are moved, suggesting that the direction of light may be important during migration. Polarized light, or light in which the rays vibrate primarily in one direction, might be especially important; experiments have shown that juvenile sockeye tend to orient their bodies parallel to polarized light in lab aquariums. Because the most intense pattern of polarized light is 90 degrees away from the sun, salmon may use it for directional cues, sharing this ability with some kinds of ants and honeybees.

However, salmon still migrate successfully in the dark and also on dull, cloudy days. Weather records show, for example, that Alaska's Bristol Bay averages 80 percent cloud cover in June, when many salmon return to fresh water. It is likely, then, that the angle of the sun isn't the only aid that salmon use to return to their spawning grounds.

Some researchers believe that tiny electrical currents in the water lead the fish toward the river mouths. Faraday's Law states that an electrical charge is produced whenever a conductor (such as sea water) passes through the earth's magnetic field. Some aquatic creatures can sense this charge: experiments with sharks have determined that they can detect even one five-billionth of a volt of electricity. Of even greater interest are experiments with Atlantic salmon that show that the fish can detect electric fields only when they are applied perpendicular to the fish's body. Theoretically, such a fish could therefore determine its orientation in major ocean currents, and this would certainly help it to find its way home.

Some animals migrate using the earth's magnetic field. It has been found, for example, that baby loggerhead turtles can determine latitude by detecting the earth's magnetic field. They can also determine longitude by measuring the intensity of the magnetic field. A number of researchers believe that salmon may have the same ability.

Other researchers have theorized that salmon may use the stars at night as navigational aids, as do some birds, or that they get directional information from the direction of waves or ocean swells.

It is not known how much of a role a salmon's sense of smell or taste plays during the ocean migration. It seems logical that as oceangoing fish approach land, the smell or taste of fresh water might lead them into river mouths. However, in one experiment, the olfactory nerves (which regulate smell) of salmon were completely severed, and yet the salmon were still able to find their way to the river mouths leading to their spawning streams. After a hundred years of research, scientists are still not able to completely explain migration.

During their final days at sea, salmon do not linger; pink salmon heading home from Alaska's Aleutian Islands average 30 miles (48 km) a day during the dash back to fresh water.

Once the salmon hit fresh water, it is most likely that a whole new set of directional aids are used to find the way home. In a famous 1954 experiment, two American biologists, Arthur Hasler and Warren Wisby, went to Issaquah Creek in Washington, where coho salmon were migrating. The nose holes of half the fish were plugged with cotton wool, and all of the fish were then taken a half-mile (0.8 km) downstream of a critical fork in the stream. The salmon whose nose holes had not been plugged all chose the correct fork and swam upstream to their natal gravels. The coho whose nose holes had been plugged were unable to choose which fork to take, and as a result made random choices between the two forks. The researchers concluded that "smell is important for salmon to find their way home."[4]

It may sound far-fetched, but due to water chemicals and the makeup of stream soils, gravels and vegetation, each stream does have its own individual smell. Famed ethologist Konrad Lorenz once investigated the same process in other animals, dubbing it "landscape imprinting." Each stock seems to develop a genetic memory for the smell of its home waters, passing it on from one generation to the next.

In addition, there may also be chemical odors from the fish themselves that linger in the water, just as the sharp smell of cigarette smoke stays in a room long after a party is over. Norwegian biologist Hans Nordeng believes that when smolts descend a river, they leave behind in the water tiny traces of sex hormones called pheromones, chemical calling cards that spawners later use to find their way home. Other researchers scoff at this notion, pointing out that the flow of water must surely wash away these pheromones within days.

However, experiments with sockeyes proved that there was indeed something in their home-stream waters that attracted them. Fish from the outlet of Great Central Lake on Vancouver Island and from Sweltzer Creek on the Fraser River were placed in laboratory tanks, and when water from their home streams was added to the tanks, the sockeyes noticeably began to swim faster. When water from other streams was added, there was no such response.

Other factors besides smell probably still wait to be discovered. It has been found that cutthroat trout, which are closely related to salmon, can find their way back to their natal streams even when their senses of sight and smell are completely blocked. Experiments with tagged chum salmon in Japan have proved that sight is not necessary for salmon to return home;

even with covered eyes, the chum had no problem returning to their natal stream.

When a human traces a familiar route, a number of aids are used: street signs, landmarks, a rough sense of the time or distance required, or the unwanted advice of a backseat driver. It is likely that salmon also use a number of different aids. And it is likely that biologists have yet to discover all of them.

The first salmon to enter fresh water on the journey home are usually chinook salmon. Alaskan chinook may show up in fresh water as early as May. Along many parts of the Pacific coast there is one spring run of chinooks and another in the fall. In the farthest north, there tends to be just one very long run. Chinooks tend to spawn the farthest distance from the ocean of all the salmon species and often prefer to use large rivers for spawning grounds. They also tend to concentrate their spawning in a relatively small number of streams and rivers; in British Columbia, half of all the chinook spawning takes place in only fourteen streams.

Sockeye salmon tend to abandon their seagoing from July through October, although some southern stocks wait until December. Sockeyes are the only salmon to occasionally spawn in submerged lake beaches rather than streams.

Pink salmon spawn as early as late July in the Yukon, but as late as October farther south. Pinks seem to be less attached to the streams of their birth than most other salmon; some have been observed spawning in a spot more than 350 miles (560 km) from their natal stream. With other species, 97 percent will spawn only in their natal stream. Efforts to transplant salmon from one stream to another often fail due to the strength of these ties.

Coho may re-enter freshwater anytime between midsummer and midwinter. They prefer to spawn in small streams close to the coast, less than 400 miles (600 km) from salt water. On their trip upstream, coho often can be seen jumping clear out of the water, even when there are no predators below or obstacles in their path. It is thought that this might be either a way for the fish to relieve tension on the stressful rush back to spawn or, less romantically, a mechanism to dislodge pesky sea lice. Strangely enough, only coho and pink salmon have been observed leaping during migration—a wondrous sight to behold.

Chum salmon are usually the slowpokes of the pack, waiting until October and November before entering coastal rivers. Some, however, start as early as August, and others as late as January. Chum seldom spawn more than 100 miles (161 km) from the ocean, though there are notable exceptions. Chum in the Amur River in Siberia, for example, swim over 300 miles (480 km) upstream. Chum in the Yukon River travel an incredible 3,200 miles (5,120 km) upstream to reach their spawning gravels, the longest trek of all for any salmon in fresh water.

Steelhead often enter fresh water months before the actual time of spawning. Different steelhead stocks choose vastly different times of the year, creating summer, winter or spring runs. The Dean River in central British Columbia's mountainous wilderness is well known as the finest summer steelhead river in North America; Oregon's Deschutes River, which runs through a parched desert, comes a close second. The contrast between the settings of the two rivers could not be more spectacular, and shows that the fish below cannot be judged by the land above.

Winter runs of steelhead are especially popular with anglers who have few other game fish to chase after the snow falls. The winter run in Washington's Sol Duc River has become famous for providing Christmas gifts that "fight back," in the form of 20-pound (9-kg) steelheads.

Upon reaching fresh water, most spawners stop eating and must live on the stored nutrients in their bodies. This is why their last days in estuarine waters are so important; they represent the spawners' last chance to feed before the long journey home. Sometimes salmon stay in these estuaries for weeks, putting on the pounds and perhaps waiting for higher water levels before heading upstream. Sockeye in British Columbia's Fraser River average a three- to six-week stay in the river's estuary before beginning the long journey home.

Strangely, though salmon rarely eat any of their natural foods during their migration upstream, they will often strike at artificial flies and lures. Migrating chum seem to prefer flies whose main body color is green. Gaudy flies like the Babine Special are eagerly snapped up by migrating steelhead. Cohos may take small flies and very small spinners. Chinook seem to prefer lures baited with

The Salmon Life Cycle: Born to Die

gobs of salmon roe, often specially cured with recipes so bizarre they make Colonel Sanders look like an amateur (my neighbor, who fishes for a living, uses a blend of borax powder, vinegar and bacon bits).

Steelhead tend to eat more on the upstream trip than most other salmon. However, the amount is still very small; one study showed that the average steelhead eats only six or seven tiny food items each day on its journey upstream, the equivalent of a full-grown man doing a hard day's work on half a slice of bread.

After spawning, steelhead may live to return to the sea and have been known to fast on their way back to salt water. One tagged steelhead went for thirty-four weeks without eating before returning to the ocean. Of those that return to the sea, between 6 and 30 percent will take a return trip back to fresh water and spawn again, making their life cycle the longest of any salmon.

The stamina of salmon on the trip home is truly amazing. Sockeyes can swim for up to twelve days with no rest at all. One sockeye at the National Marine Fisheries Service lab in Bonneville, Oregon, climbed an artificial fish ladder for five days with no rest—an artificial climb of over 6,600 feet (2,000 m). Such exertion takes its toll; sockeye returning to Stuart Lake in British Columbia were found to have used up 96 percent of their body fat *en route*.

Of course, even salmon can get too tired to paddle on occasion; at these times they nip into side streams or flat back eddies for a well-deserved snooze. Steelhead like to rest in the first quiet stretch of water above a set of rapids. Chinook and coho prefer to hole up in deep pools, especially during the late afternoon or early evening. Chum are fond of holding over shallow sandbars in water less than 3 feet (1 m) deep. The areas just upstream of these resting sites are favorite spots for hordes of eager anglers, who hit the jackpot in the early morning when the fish begin to move upstream.

Another way for a fish to conserve energy is to swim closely behind other fish—the same logic used by drivers of Volkswagens who follow huge Kenworth trucks on freeways. Experiments have shown that maneuvering behind larger fish can reduce drag in the water by one-half. Thus, the tight schooling of salmon is probably not only for defensive purposes, but also to save energy.

Upon reaching fresh water, the beautiful salmon begins to transform from Dr. Jekyll into Mr. Hyde. The abdomens of females begin to swell, and their gums recede to expose their teeth. Males tend to gain a vicious-looking hooked upper jaw and a deformed-looking humped back, most obvious in the pink salmon. The humped back of the males probably helps females survive, as predators are more likely to snatch up the males whose humps protrude above the water's surface.

A male's color may also change from a bright silver to a dull green or purple, or bright red in the case of sockeyes. The color often intensifies with distance from the sea, and indicates the male's readiness to breed. Females turn a dull green or dull red. This color change is triggered by the increased activity of sex hormones. Even kokanees, the land-locked form of sockeyes, gain bright red coats at spawning time, proving that color change is not related to water salinity, as was once thought.

Unfortunately, the flashy new coat is highly attractive to predators as well; one study in Alaska found that hungry bears preferred the more brightly colored male salmon to the dull-colored females. In the world of the salmon, equality of the sexes isn't always desirable.

The skin of the spawner also thickens at this time, in order to protect the fish from the hazards of the long trip ahead. The skin of chum salmon thickens so much in fact that it is sometimes sold as "salmon leather."

The final step in this process is for the bodies of the male salmon to widen, making them more difficult for other males to grab during disputes over females.

By the time a spawner reaches its home gravels, it looks moth-eaten and tattered. Battles with rapids, waterfalls, jagged boulders and lucky escapes from predators all combine to change the flashy silver coat of the adult salmon into a ratty thrift store reject.

Adding to this carnage is the natural deterioration of the salmon's body, which now accelerates rapidly. The salmon's pituitary and adrenal glands speed up their activity and the salmon begins to literally fall apart. Inside the fish, fatty deposits begin to accumulate in the arteries, an ailment commonly known as hardening of the arteries in both humans and fish. On the outside of the fish, the rotting flesh is often covered with white wisps of fungus. In its last few weeks of life, the noble salmon, King of the Pacific, is really nothing more than the living dead.

Despite the many hazards, a salmon's last trip home is often a speedy one. On Oregon's Rogue River, the average steelhead takes twenty-one days to travel 60 miles (96 km) upstream. Sockeye in the Fraser River have been clocked traveling 315 miles (500 km) in only eighteen days.

On the way upriver, some salmon duck into side ponds or streams to avoid heavy silt runs in the river. Some of these fish can then become disoriented and never make it home, like tourists who take a wrong turn and end up in the wrong part of town.

...And to the stream
But many salmon do make it to the mouth of their natal stream, where they then often bunch up like cars in a rush-hour traffic jam. The next step is to wait for their sexual hormones to trigger the perfect moment for spawning. In the males, tubules inside the testes begin to thicken in preparation for the release of sperm. Within the females, precious eggs begin to ripen and separate. In some species, the lateral line of the female darkens, a come-on to males, showing she is ready to spawn.

Once the salmon reach the streams of their birth, the passion play of courtship begins. Males compete with other males through threat displays and fights, grabbing each other's jaws or the narrow "wrist" area just in front of the tail fin. Some will open their mouths wide or spread out their fins in an attempt to look as large and awesome as possible. Most will turn sideways to display their length, but some will actually tear chunks of flesh out of another fish in an effort to win a partner.

When an eager male salmon finds an interested female, he will cruise alongside her and slightly above her. Occasionally, his body will quiver all over with a sensation that looks like a shiver. The movement causes vibrations in the water that some suggest the female finds appealing. Pushing his luck further, the male will then slide over the female's back, another move that female salmon seem to enjoy. The males' bright colors and sensual movements appear to be an important part of the reproduction process.

In one experiment, a group of female sockeyes were separated from the males, and without the visual stimulus of the male salmon, it took several days longer for them to dig nests and lay their eggs.

The females cruise along the gravelly bottom of the stream, looking for just the right spot to lay their eggs. Each species is picky about choosing a certain diameter of stream-bottom gravel, and each have choice nesting spots, usually the first spots to be grabbed by females. Steelhead tend to prefer gravel around 0.75 inches (19 mm) in diameter; many big female chinooks like gravel over twice that size. In general terms, the bigger the egg, the larger the gravel that is chosen.

The nest sites must be clean and free from silt, so that water can flow freely around the eggs. Popular nest spots include the choppy water found just in front of logs or rocks, where the rough water creates an increased amount of oxygen to sustain eggs.

Water temperature is also an important spawning factor. Steelhead, for example, prefer spawning waters at 55°F (13°C); sockeye like it a little warmer, about 59°F (15°C). Anything warmer may speed up body metabolism and cause heat stress. Pinks seem to be the least fussy when it comes to water temperatures (they sometimes don't even worry about salinity either: a small population of pinks in Fraser Lake, on Alaska's Kodiak Island, never leave fresh water at all).

Fights between females over nest sites are common, with bigger females biting the gill plates of smaller fish, or tearing at their tail in order to win a particularly attractive nesting spot.

When a female has chosen a good spot, she then turns on her side and, with sweeping motions of her tail, digs out a nest. If another male enters the nest area during this time, her mate will diligently chase it away. The nest may be up to 18 inches (46 cm) deep and 3 feet (1 m) long in the case of big female chinook salmon. The average sockeye nest is an oval scoop 40 inches (100 cm) long, 33 inches (83 cm) wide, and 3.5 inches (9 cm) deep. The digging may take hours, or even days, depending on the nature of the stream bed. By the time she is finished, the female's tail fin is usually frayed and torn from the aggressive sweeping motion used to create her nest.

The
Salmon
Life
Cycle:
Born
to Die

Males have also been known to dig nests, though these are never actually used. Biologists believe that this is a type of displacement behavior—an action that serves no purpose but to relieve tension or stress. Humans chew their fingernails; male salmon dig nests.

When the female's nest is almost finished, she bends her body into a U-shape and lets her anal fin drop into the nest. This twisting of her body seems to excite the male, who hovers closer. Upon his approach, she drops her anal fin again into the nest. Often their mouths open from the tension, although less romantic researchers have suggested that the gaping mouths may actually help hold the salmon in place in the current. Then, with a delicate quiver, the female drops thousands of eggs into the nest. Her mate spurts out his sperm, known as milt, in a milky cloud either at the same time or shortly thereafter.

The entire sex act from release of eggs to deposition of sperm lasts less than twenty seconds. Each batch of eggs typically contains 500 to 5,000 eggs. Female steelheads may lay up to 40,000 eggs. Each burst of male milt contains about 50 million sperm.

Many of the eggs and sperm will wash away in the current, sometimes avidly gobbled up by other fish.

Upon spotting a cloud of sperm, other males, especially smaller males who have not attracted a mate, will often rush in and try desperately to release their own sperm over the female's eggs. The mated male will aggressively repel these fishy gigolos so that few succeed. Studies of pink and chum salmon found that most small males still had lots of unused sperm at the end of the spawning season. Male salmon can breed more than once, but shortly after their sperm is depleted, they will die.

Very rarely, males of another salmon species will zip in and successfully fertilize the eggs. Pinks, for example, can breed with chums, creating a fertile hybrid that tends to have a very short life cycle. There are also hybrids of pinks and chinooks (logically enough called "pinooks"), which are found in the Great Lakes area, that can reach up to 14 pounds (6 kg).

The massive quantities of sperm and egg fluids that fill the water at spawning time create a sex hormone-filled soup whose potency must overwhelm the salmon's acute sense of smell.

Perhaps this is why the spawning grounds become a boiling cauldron of activity, the reproductive equivalent of a shark's feeding frenzy.

Once the male has released his sperm, the female begins to carefully cover the eggs, fanning the gravel over them with her tail. The male's sperm will survive for less than a minute in the frigid water, and fertilization must therefore occur quickly. The sperm become very active, darting around the pile of eggs. At the top of each egg is a tiny hole called a micropyle, and out of each micropyle oozes a chemical agent that attracts the sperm. In order for fertilization to occur, one sperm must enter the micropyle of an egg, penetrate the thinner membrane and unite with the nucleus of the egg.

After the egg is fertilized, it will absorb water and swell up to 30 percent its original size, effectively closing the micropyle to other sperm. Each egg is slightly sticky, to avoid being washed away, and after fertilization it will harden for further protection.

In the meantime, the female salmon, immediately after laying her first batch of eggs and covering them up, begins to dig another nest. Usually the next nest is just upstream of the first one, so that the gravel she scoops out from the second nest will drift downstream and help cover the first batch of eggs. This set of nests that a salmon creates is called a redd. In creating a redd, a female will often dig up another female's redd, destroying the other's eggs in the process. Whether this is by accident or intentional is anybody's guess—there would certainly be a genetic advantage in the bigger and stronger females destroying other's nests, but chances are that the destruction is accidental.

A female may dig from one to five redds, laying eggs in each, before she finally reaches exhaustion and dies. Sometimes she has enough energy to guard her redds for a few days, adding gravel to cover them and chasing off other salmon, but eventually she joins the rest of the dying salmon, which lie rocking in the wake of the river, awaiting death. For female sockeyes, the average interval between spawning and death is nine to ten days. Spawned-out adults are known as "kelts," a term stolen from the lingo of Atlantic salmon biologists.

If the female dies before her mate, the male will try to pair

The
Salmon
Life
Cycle:
Born
to Die

again. Life is a lottery for the salmon, who must stack all the odds they can in their favor in order to win. For every 4,000 eggs produced by a pair of salmon, only 2 will survive all the rigors of life to reach adulthood, return and spawn.

I've noticed that often, just before death, exhausted salmon will struggle to the center of streams, where the flow of water is strongest, thus pushing life-giving oxygen over failing gills. Even hours from death, the spark of life can be observed trying vainly to burn on. It appears to be mainly groups of males that do this; I have observed very few females gathering in this manner.

Finally the salmon can swim no more, and they roll helplessly onto their sides as their life processes gear down and finally stop. To me, this is the saddest time to observe salmon, for the sight of thousands of magnificent creatures gasping their last cannot help but move you. They have come so far, and gone through so much, their last hours seem a second-rate ending.

But from this massive die-off springs life. Life in the form of a new generation of salmon, but also life in the form of a long list of scavengers that will feed upon the dead salmon littering the rivers after spawning. Bears, gulls, herons and eagles are all part of the hungry hordes that descend upon the river to enjoy a salmon dinner.

As a direct result of this, one of the best spots in North America to watch eagles is the Chilkat Eagle Preserve, located 15 miles (24 km) north of Haines, Alaska. Between October and January, more than 3,000 bald eagles gather at upwellings of warm water in the preserve to feast upon dead and dying chum salmon. The 49,000-acre (20,000-ha) preserve, created in 1982, has attracted biologists and wildlife photographers from around the world.

In Canada, a similar annual gathering occurs near Squamish, British Columbia, where a record 3,701 eagles were counted on January 9, 1994—the largest one-day eagle count ever recorded anywhere. In October 1996, the provincial government announced that the area would be set aside as the Brackendale Eagle Reserve.

In Alaska, two areas have gained fame as excellent viewing sites for huge grizzlies attracted by fall salmon runs. The McNeil River State Game Sanctuary, on the coast southwest of Anchorage,

Alaska, is the best known. Runs of chum, with occasional chinooks, pinks and sockeyes, draw hundreds of the big bears each year. From a viewing site overlooking McNeil Falls, as many as sixty-seven grizzlies have been seen at one time. Southwest of Juneau, on Admiralty Island, Pack Creek is the site of a similar gathering of salmon-seeking bears. Twenty to thirty bears may be seen at one time at Pack Creek; daily visits are limited to twenty-four lucky humans.

It is not only scavenging animals that benefit from dead salmon; nutrients from the salmons' deteriorating bodies also fertilize streamside trees and shrubs. Studies in the state of Washington have found that the nitrogen in salmon carcasses is unique and can be traced as it is used by other animals and plants.

In some Washington spawning streams, 18 percent of the nitrogen found in streamside hemlocks, salmonberry and devil's club comes from decayed salmon. In addition, 20 to 30 percent of the body mass of insects collected on Washington's Snoqualmie River originated from salmon carcasses.

In coastal British Columbia, biologists have found that bears haul much larger quantities of salmon farther into the woods than was ever before imagined. University of Victoria biologists have found bear-hauled salmon up to 492 feet (150 m) away from streams. As a result, scientists have measured the amounts of salmon left on the forest floor and found them to be equivalent to 3,563 pounds of commercial fertilizer per acre (4,000 kg/ha). Much of the impressive tree growth alongside salmon streams can thus be attributed to the salmon themselves.

In yet another of nature's circles, salmon carcasses are also an important source of food for juvenile salmon. Juvenile salmon grow almost twice as fast in streams rich in salmon carcasses as in those without. In fact, the breakdown of salmon carcasses is so significant to the continued health and growth of salmon populations that, in the fall of 1996, Washington state salmon hatcheries started placing a limited number of these carcasses along rivers in order to supplement both the fish and the surrounding greenery.

In the past biologists have considered spawners as only a primary source of eggs; now they have also begun to realize that they are also an important source of nourishment for dozens of plants and animals. As a result, they have begun to lower the commercial harvest rate accordingly.

The last significant contribution that salmon carcasses make to the ecosystem is to increase the amount of plankton in the water for future salmon to feed upon. In this way salmon fuel an intricate cycle of life that rolls on fluidly and endlessly. Only one obstacle is severe enough to affect that cycle or even stop it altogether: the intervention of humankind.

5. OF FISH AND MEN

"We do not own ... the sparkle of the water ... Every part of this Earth is sacred."
CHIEF SEATHL, 1855

To most people, Alaska represents the unreachable attic of the continent, the last refuge for dozens of beleaguered species. Tragically, the very wealth of Alaska's natural resources has drawn many wishing to exploit those resources. The sad truth is that not only do those natural resources sustain the continent, they also sustain a variety of nearly extinct species. The effects of exploitation upon salmon, for example, have been tragic.

That first salmon run that I watched, in a pristine Alaskan stream back in 1971, took place in water that was as clear as a tear, running through a picture-perfect valley. That same stream is now the color of light chocolate; the grit in the water grates against your teeth, and against your soul. The valley walls are now splattered with clearcut patches that have bared the earth to the rains, allowing slurries of mud to carry the precious soil into the streams. Without the shade of riparian trees, the water of that stream is now warm to the taste; the delicious chill born in upstream glaciers has disappeared. And no salmon have spawned in the stream now for at least a dozen years.

If David Letterman were to do a list of the "Top Five Ways to

Destroy the Salmon" (or "Stupid Salmon Tricks"), it would run something like this: 5. Cut the forests down around the streams; 4. Build dams across salmon streams; 3. Add cows and runoff to the water; 2. Pollute the waters; and 1. Overfish the resource.

LOGGING

When Captain James Cook first sailed into west-coast waters in 1778, he decided to strip coastal valleys of their huge firs, which he used as spars for his wooden ships. For the next two centuries, this "cut and run" attitude prevailed, with devastating results.

Poor logging practices can result in a world of woes to salmon, not to mention all other living species. Clearcutting, by definition, removes all forest cover, leading to landslides or mud flows that all too often result in clogged streams along valley bottoms.

Increases in stream silt levels can also be a result of logging. At Jim Creek in Montana, scientists with the U.S. Forest Service and Montana Department of Fish, Wildlife and Parks measured silt levels prior to and after logging along the valley. The average silt level in the creek above the logging area did not change from 1988 to 1990. The silt level below the logging area increased to 50 percent. Experiments with both trout and salmon eggs have shown that silt levels as low as 30 percent can reduce the number of eggs that hatch by one-half.

Another result of logging is the removal of streamside trees. Without their shade, water temperatures can increase significantly above levels at which salmon prefer to spawn.

Bark from logging operations will often eventually wash downhill, where it then accumulates in streams. When rivers and lakes are used as transportation corridors for log booms, a tremendous amount of bark may also fall into the water. The bark can then smother salmon eggs, or decay and rob the eggs of oxygen.

In some places, loggers build "splash dams," temporary structures used to store water until it can be suddenly released to float the logs downstream. These dams can block crucial migration routes to spawning salmon, and the sudden flood of water often washes away precious eggs.

The longest-running fish-and-forestry project in North America is the Carnation Creek study on the west coast of Vancouver

Island. The study began in 1970 and is still in operation today. Carnation Creek supports populations of coho, chum and steelhead, and has been intensely monitored both before and after logging operations. Biologists have compiled a long list of negative effects on fish populations as the result of logging operations; these include higher stream temperatures, decreased numbers of aquatic insects, delayed alevin emergence from stream-bed gravels, smaller alevin size and a 50 percent decrease in the egg-to-fry survival rate.

Pro-forestry forces often allege that these types of problems are a thing of the past. But research proves otherwise. In 1995, the government of British Columbia released the results of an independent consultant's report on logging practices on Vancouver Island. Of fifty-three fish-bearing streams inspected, two-thirds had been harmed by sloppy logging practices.

DAM CONSTRUCTION

A 1906 report on a Native wooden fish weir on British Columbia's Babine River described it as a magnificent structure, but impenetrable to fish. In the years to come, European settlers improved upon this idea by creating massive structures of earth and concrete that put power first and fish last.

Aside from creating an obvious physical obstacle to salmon, dams also harm salmon populations in a number of different ways; for example, the whirling blades of the dam turbines can easily slice a live salmon to pieces. Many salmon smolts that attempt to swim through dam turbines die in the process. And most smolts that try to swim over dam spillways also lose their lives.

Another negative effect of dams is that the water stored behind them often becomes overheated. This dramatic increase in water temperature can kill delicate juvenile salmon. Fish that do survive often die from the increased oxygen and nitrogen levels that occur in water below the dams (caused by the dissolution of these gases as water travels over a spillway). The effect these gases have upon salmon results in something called "bubble disease," similar to the "bends" suffered by human divers. Up to 90 percent of juvenile salmon that make it over dams later die from bubble disease.

Sometimes smolts will waste days trying to get through,

around, or even over dams. The increased travel time caused by these obstacles can cause fish to lose their urge to migrate. It can even stress them to the point of death.

Despite the documented evidence that fish and dams don't mix, politicians have been slow to drop the idea of cheap hydro power. In 1955, B.C. Hydro proposed a 750-foot (228-m)-high dam on the Fraser River, the greatest salmon river on the continent. The dam was to be located across Moran Canyon, just above the town of Lillooet, approximately 185 miles (280 km) upstream from the mouth of the Fraser River. It would have blocked migration routes to salmon from Lillooet to Prince George, thus jeopardizing dozens of salmon stocks throughout central British Columbia. The Canadian Fisheries Department filed an objection, but it was public pressure that finally forced B.C. Hydro to drop the idea in 1971 for the sake of the salmon. No one has since dared to be so thoughtless.

In the United States, twelve years of legal action by concerned environmentalists finally resulted in legislation aimed at protecting salmon from the disasters caused by dams. In a 1994 decision, the Federal Energy Regulatory Commission (FERC) was ordered to examine any future hydroelectric project that may affect the well-being of salmon. This decision, however, came too late for many rivers.

Take the Elwha Dam, for example. When the dam was built on the Elwha River in Washington's Olympic Peninsula in 1913, there weren't any regulations requiring the placement of fish ladders to help the salmon around the barrier. Biologists believe that, at one time, up to 390,000 spawners used this river system each year; now only a few survive. The 105-foot (32-m)-high structure hurt the river's salmon runs so dramatically that a bill was passed in 1992 to remove the dam. Politicians have stalled this bill, balking at the $113-million price tag. Conservationists argue that, aside from restoring the salmon runs, the removal of the concrete calamity would create 450 local jobs in recreation and tourism, some of which might go to the beleaguered Lower Elwha S'Kallam tribe who once depended on the salmon for a major portion of their food supply.

One of the most dammed rivers on the continent is the

Columbia River, which has over a dozen dams on its main branch alone. At least another hundred dams straddle its various tributaries. No other river has suffered from such an orgy of dam-building.

According to a Colville tribal legend, at one time there was a large lake in the spot presently occupied by the Columbia River. Between this lake and the sea was a high mountain chain. When wise old Coyote saw salmon gathering in the ocean, he dug a hole through the mountains to give the salmon access to the lake. The salmon swam up the new river that was created, and Coyote's people have had salmon to eat ever since. Then came the white man.

When explorers Meriwether Lewis and William Clark traveled the Columbia River in 1805, they reported seeing great quantities of salmon. One hundred years later, those vast numbers of salmon were in serious trouble. The Columbia River once hosted runs of 10 million to 16 million salmon each year; by the 1970s, this figure had dropped below 2.5 million. The peak Columbia River commercial salmon and steelhead catch in recent years occurred in 1941, when 2,112,500 fish were caught. The 1995 catch numbered only 68,000 fish—a staggering 97 percent drop in five decades.

At one time the dams along the Columbia River provided a third of all the hydroelectric power in the United States, a source of power for people from Seattle to San Francisco. This power, however, has cost the salmon their valuable habitat. Many Columbia River salmon stocks have never recovered.

One of the most famous of the Columbia River dams is the Grand Coulee Dam, the construction of which destroyed 70 percent of the spawning grounds for spring chinook in the area. In Idaho's Snake River, one of the Columbia's main tributaries, the sockeye and chinook have almost entirely disappeared. Both species are now listed as endangered under the Endangered Species Act. According to the National Marine Fisheries Service, today between 67 and 88 percent of the fall juvenile Snake River chinook are killed by dams on the Columbia River. Wild coho salmon no longer run in the upper Columbia River and are also rare in the lower Columbia River.

Increasingly we are realizing that power for the people comes at a very high price to the natural world.

AGRICULTURE

Many of the streams found in the San Francisco area were great steelhead waters in the early 1900s, before humans flooded into the state. When the first settlers arrived, the dry lands of southern California needed water, and so many northern salmon streams were diverted for irrigation. No one stopped to consider how much the salmon might need that same water. By the 1920s, a number of steelhead stocks had been totally destroyed. By 1929, only one-tenth of the original chinook spawning grounds in the San Joaquin and Sacramento Rivers remained. Today, the winter chinook in California's Sacramento River is on the threatened-species list.

In Oregon, the rich farmland surrounding Tillamook Bay is home to 25,000 dairy cattle, which produce more than 300,000 gallons (1 million liters) of waste every day. Much of this muck eventually ends up in the bay, which, as a result, must be closed to shellfish harvesting for two or three months every year. Local fishers report that many of the salmon that used to feed in this bay have now gone elsewhere, as they are unable to feed in water that is clouded by cow manure.

Streamside ranches and feed lots pose some of the biggest obstacles to salmon conservation. Cattle from these operations are often allowed to wade into streams, crushing salmon eggs, and raising silt and waste levels in the water.

I once watched a herd of cattle cross a salmon stream in the rolling ranch country of western Oregon. At least a hundred animals plunged into the water and were pushed to the other side on the annual trek to their winter pasture. The stream they had entered had been crystal clear; the stream they left behind was a muddy quagmire. Three years later, not a single salmon had spawned in that stream.

POLLUTION

Because salmon require cold, clear water, they are often among the first fish to show the effects of water degradation, the river's version of a canary in a coal mine.

One of the most crucial points in the salmon's life cycle is the time spent in inshore estuaries, where the salmon feed before migrating upstream. Unfortunately, these areas are also subjected to high levels of human use, and all too often the waters become tainted as a result. The greater Vancouver area, for example, pumps out 200 million gallons (750 million liters) of sewage *every day* into the Fraser River estuary. And, both north and south of the estuary, there are a number of small oceanside communities which still do not adequately treat their sewage before dumping it into the sea, although most of these situations have been identified and are presently slated for upgrading. However, because of the combined effects of sewage, urban sprawl, industrial pollution and agricultural runoff, in 1996 the Outdoor Recreation Council named the Fraser River British Columbia's most endangered river.

Upriver, pulp-and-paper mills are some of the worst offenders when it comes to the pollution of salmon streams. Heated effluents from these plants may cause mats of algae downstream, mats that can smother salmon eggs and remove crucial oxygen from the water.

Wood fiber from the pulping process is another form of water pollution that consumes oxygen as it decays, thus killing salmon eggs and fry. High levels of toxic chemicals from pulp mills are also sometimes dumped into the water, shortening fish longevity as well as their ability to spawn. One of the worst such groups of chemicals are dioxins, organic compounds that can cause impaired reproduction and birth defects in a variety of wildlife. In many areas, legislation aimed at reducing dioxin pollution did not appear until the early 1990s, far too late for many salmon stocks. In British Columbia, dioxin levels have dropped by 98 percent since 1990 and the province hopes to be dioxin-free by the year 2000.

Industrial wastes are another unwelcome addition to some rivers. In the 1970s, coastal waters off Japan became so polluted that people were warned not to eat locally caught salmon.

In more recent times, the 1989 spill of 11 million gallons (42 million liters) of crude oil into Alaska's pristine Prince William Sound had devastating effects on the wildlife of the area. More than 300 salmon streams enter into Prince William Sound. The year after the spill, fishers noted that the young pink salmon were smaller than normal and that many salmon eggs had been killed. The long-term effects have yet to be seen.

Perhaps the Bella Coola tribes had the best idea of all: any member caught throwing garbage into a stream at spawning time was put to death.

COMMERCIAL OVERFISHING

In addition to human waste, human greed has also taken its toll on salmon populations. One of the most productive salmon rivers in the United States used to be the Columbia River. But by 1877, more than 1,000 gillnets and fish traps were set in the river. Within a dozen years, many of the salmon runs in the Columbia River were in serious decline. More recently, in Washington's Puget Sound, so many sockeye salmon were trapped in a 2,000-foot (609-m)-long fish trap that tens of thousands of them died—destroying a whole sockeye run in the process.

Today, a bewildering tangle of state, provincial and federal laws regulate the fishing industry. In 1980, Roderick Haig-Brown wrote that "the fisherman's only real competition is with his quarry."[1] Twenty years later, the real competition seems to be between fishers and government.

The central question of how many fish should be harvested each year is never answered to everyone's satisfaction. Estimating a salmon run is a tricky business; Herman Savikko, a biologist with the Alaska Department of Fish and Game, admits, "We're wrong more than 50 percent of the time."[2] This inaccuracy has led to countless cases of commercial overfishing.

One of the first tools used by prehistoric man was the fish hook, a rudimentary tool that managed to catch only a limited number of fish. In the centuries since its invention (by some nameless angler), fishing has become devastatingly efficient.

Commercial fishers now use one of three main types of salmon-fishing techniques: trollers drag lures in the water, in a large-scale version of sport angling; gillnetters use long nets that grab salmon by the gills; and seiners use a circular net that closes with a purse string at the bottom.

Thousands of fishers use each of these techniques each year in the mistaken belief that the sea's bounty is endless. Early on, a few voices began to be raised about the rate at which Pacific salmon were being fished. Unfortunately nobody listened.

For most game species, wildlife managers recommend that 4 to 10 percent of the total population is the maximum sustainable harvest rate each year. And yet commercial fishers consistently take huge harvests many times those figures.

Fisheries biologist W.E. Ricker studied Canadian Department of Fisheries and Oceans (DFO) statistics and reported in 1987 that the sockeye catch during 1930 to 1934 "is estimated to have been 91 to 94 percent."[3] And, more recently, the DFO's 1995 South Coast Coho Integrated Management Plan report reported that, by 1985, coho harvest rates reached as high as 85 percent.

In 1990, 90 percent of the pinks entering Prince William Sound in Alaska were taken by commercial fishers before the fish even had a chance to enter their spawning streams.

Three years later, the United Nations Food and Agriculture Organization stated that the North Pacific and sixteen other major world fishing areas had fishing levels which met or exceeded their natural limits. Again, nobody listened.

Today, most fisheries managers try to keep the salmon harvest level down to about 30 percent. Many biologists, however, believe that even that figure is too generous.

It should also be noted that some of the damage that results from intensive commercial fishing is not obvious and is therefore rarely accounted for in determining adequate fishing quotas. It has been found, for example, that the stress experienced by a salmon caught in a gillnet for even a few minutes will likely cause so much damage that the salmon will die before it has the chance to spawn.

And finally there is the controversy over the damage caused by catch-and-release sport fishing. The theory behind catch-and-release fishing makes sense: many anglers truly enjoy the chase more than the catch itself (in 1496, Dame Juliana Berners cheerfully noted that, even if an angler doesn't catch a fish, he has had a "holsom walke" and inhaled the "swete ayre" of the wild in the process). When anglers are allowed to catch fish and then release them, the anglers still get their sport and the rivers still keep their fish.

Unfortunately, in real life it isn't so simple. The truth is that many fish hooked and released later die from the injuries or stress caused by being caught. The percentage varies between 0.5 and 90, depending on the species and the area. One crucial factor is where the fish is hooked; the majority of young chinook and coho salmon caught in the gills or associated blood vessels later die from these injuries.

In many cases, a fish dies after being caught and released because of a very high concentration of lactic acid in the fish's bloodstream—the same stuff that makes human legs or arms ache after exercise. The interesting point is that these high levels are reached gradually, with buildup continuing hours after the initial stress of being caught. Thus, many fish die two or three hours after capture. The angler who releases a fish and happily sees it swim away is self-deluding; three hours later that fish may well be dead.

There is also the handling factor. Many salmon are quite delicate; a fish released by a ham-fisted fisher often dies later of internal injuries or of infections caused by a loss of its protective slime. Even removing a fish from the water for too long can hurt a fish's internal organs.

Fishers can show more respect for the fish they catch through more careful handling and the use of barbless hooks. But there will always be a number of salmon killed by catch-and-release angling. However, in the big picture of Pacific salmon management and conservation, the sport catch is really a minor factor. More than 400 million salmon are caught each year by commercial fishers; the sport catch is less than 1 million fish. Compared with the population ravages caused by commercial overfishing, the effects of sport anglers, whether they use catch-and-release techniques or not, amount to only a few fish out of a very, very big barrel.

6. TO SAVE THE SALMON

"If we could bring the salmon back like before, the people would be happy."

YAKIMA CHIEF LEVI GEORGE, 1990

Archeologists have found that many Native tribes in the Pacific Northwest were heavily dependent upon salmon catches as a means of survival as early as 9,000 years ago. Indeed, to some tribes, the flood of salmon that arrived each fall meant the difference between life and death. A crude net of bark could bring in enough food to feed a family for a year. Dried or smoked salmon was the prime winter fare for many a tribe.

Often the salmon was smoked until it was rock-hard; Joseph McGillivray, a trader with the Hudson's Bay Company, reported in 1827 that "it actually files the teeth to the very gums."[1] Salmon eggs were considered a particular delicacy; long before New York socialites discovered the delights of sturgeon caviar, coastal Native peoples made their own version from the eggs of salmon. Eggs were placed in cedar baskets or into the cleaned stomach of a deer, and the whole mess was then kneaded daily until it fermented into a gooey, nutritious treat.

When European settlers discovered salmon, they pursued them with such vengeance and greed that they sparked the decline of many a species across North America. By the early 1800s, the Fraser River was the world's largest salmon fishery.

Today, vast armies of ships swarm over the near-shore Pacific waters, hauling in millions of salmon each year. The Pacific salmon catch is worth over $1 billion annually. The largest Canadian catch is from British Columbia. Over 70 percent of that salmon is exported each year. The largest commercial haul in the United States comes from Alaska, and the bulk of those fish go to Japan.

As the demand for salmon has grown, so has the demand for scientific facts on which to base conservation work and fishing quotas.

Much of the early scientific work on salmon was performed by biologist Charles H. Gilbert, of Stanford University. Gilbert was the first biologist to discover the meaning of the rings on a salmon's scales. He was also the first to determine the life spans of the various species, and one of the first scientists to study the homing instinct of salmon. He died in the midst of his studies, but his work was carried on by W.A. Clemens, a Canadian biologist with the Pacific Biological Station in Nanaimo, British Columbia.

While the scientific world was amassing data on the various salmon species, government authorities began to note the alarming declines of the annual catches reported to them. They recorded, for example, that 1,172,507 cases of canned sockeye were packed in the United States and Canada in 1897, dropping to only 372,020 cases in 1903. Six years later scientists recommended that the fish be tagged in order to determine just what was behind this rapid decline. (See appendix B, C, D)

It was until 1916, however, that some of the first Pacific salmon to be tagged were traced by scientists. This took place in the Columbia River, and the clipping revealed that many species of salmon were not making it home to spawn.

Investigations into the causes of these losses led to the formation in 1937 of the International Pacific Salmon Fisheries Commission, composed of three designates from the United States and three from Canada. Their mission was to rebuild the salmon fishery. The race to save the salmon had begun.

From 1937 to the 1960s, the prime tool used in salmon conservation was the hatchery. Since the greatest number of natural losses in the salmon's life cycle occur during the egg and larval stage, it makes sense to artificially improve the survival rate during these times.

The first salmon hatchery in the United States opened in 1872, on the McCloud River in northern California. In its first year of operations, the primitive hatchery, housed in a rickety wooden cabin, produced 30,000 salmon eggs, which were shipped to New Jersey in a misguided attempt to introduce Pacific salmon to the east. Over 24,000 of these precious eggs were lost in transit, a tragic beginning to the hatchery business. The first hatchery in the Columbia River basin opened in 1877. Canada's first hatchery opened in 1883 at Bon Accord on the Fraser River.

The premise of hatcheries is simple: maintain perfect conditions and more eggs will hatch. Unfortunately, many of the early hatcheries opened before much was known about salmon propagation.

Feeding techniques in the early hatcheries were especially primitive. It was common for such bizarre fare as horse meat and condemned beef to be forced upon hatchery salmon. In some hatcheries, rotting cows' heads were hung over the water, and the maggots that fell into the water were snapped up by eager salmon fingerlings. It is no surprise that disease and low survival rates were common among these fish.

Finally, an experiment in 1940 in which salmon were force fed a yucky mix of sheep liver and wheat meal convinced biologists that more nutritious foods were required. Over the following two decades, scientists raced to find better ways of building bigger salmon.

By the 1960s, science had finally reached the hatcheries, and vitamin-rich pelleted foods became the norm. Survival rates soared, death rates dropped and many of the hatcheries became efficient fish factories. Washington's Cowlitz hatchery, for example, produced 28 million eggs annually at its peak.

Flushed with success, gung-ho fisheries biologists sent both

To Save the Salmon

eggs and fingerlings to rivers across North America; many of these rivers had never before seen a salmon.

One of the first such transplants turned out to be a lucky accident. In 1956, fishery workers accidentally dumped hundreds of British Columbia pinks *en route* to Hudson Bay into Lake Superior. The fish survived and thrived, spreading to all of the other Great Lakes. Ironically enough, the fish that eventually were transplanted to Hudson Bay failed to survive and reproduce.

In 1966 and 1967, cohos and chinooks from Oregon and Washington hatcheries were introduced to Lake Michigan and Lake Superior, starting important sport fisheries. Similar attempts to introduce sport salmon to Newfoundland and Maine failed.

There were even attempts to introduce Pacific salmon to such far-flung sites as Europe, Hawaii, Australia, Argentina, Chile, Mexico and New Zealand. Of all these, only the last was successful, and anglers on the South Island of New Zealand today can still catch salmon whose ancestors began as eggs in American hatcheries.

Today, hatchery fish account for approximately 25 percent of the total Pacific catch reported by Alaskan commercial fishers. In Canada, 12 percent of the catch began life in a hatchery.

In the United States, more than 50 million hatchery-raised salmon are released each year. In some local areas, hatchery fish are an important part of the sport-angler harvest. In Washington, for example, 85 percent of the steelhead taken by sport anglers are hatchery fish.

In Japan, where severe overfishing has destroyed most wild stocks, hatchery fish now account for over 75 percent of the commercial catch. Japan releases over 2 billion hatchery-raised salmon each year, 93 percent of which are chum. Russia releases another 1 billion chum annually.

Altogether, over 5 billion hatchery salmon are released each year in the North Pacific, an amazing addition to our wild world.

However, hatchery fish have many problems. The differences between a hatchery fish and a wild fish are similar to the differences between a domestic dog and a wolf. If you were to take the average dog out into the wild and leave it there, chances are it would die within a month. A domesticated dog doesn't know how to hunt, how to avoid predators, how to treat an injury or where to hole up in a storm. If it tries to join a wild wolf pack or mate with a wild wolf, it will be killed instantly by the other wolves. Dogs are simply not meant to live in the wild. Neither are fish that are bred in hatcheries.

Wild fish have locked within their genes the secrets to survival. Hatchery fish do not. First, hatchery fish are less resistant to disease in the wild and may even introduce disease caught in the hatcheries to the outside fish. Second, if hatchery fish mate with wild fish, the genetic purity of the wild species is diluted, and the offspring may not spawn successfully. And, perhaps most important, both hatchery fish and the offspring of hatchery fish and wild fish matings tend to have a lower survival rate in the wild.

Consider the way hatchery fish are raised. They are kept in crowded tanks, and are used to aggressively rushing in to grab their share of the food. They have no experience with predators, and are used to the presence of humans. What happens when these fish are trucked out to the wild and suddenly released?

At first, they continue to crowd together in the water, and thus make excellent targets for predators. When they fight for a share of the available food, they take food from the wild fish. Often the hatchery fish win these fights, as they may be five times the size of their wild cousins. Their aggression causes an increased mortality overall, and eventually a decrease in the wild gene pool. It is in that gene pool, however, that exists the secret to salmon migration and survival, the keys to the wild kingdom. Without those keys, the whole salmon population suffers.

It should also be noted that many anglers swear that hatchery fish lack the fighting spirit of wild fish (due largely to their being conditioned to being handled) and are not near as tasty (due to their bland scientific diet in the hatchery).

For all of these reasons, there has evolved a fervid backlash among the fishing fraternity against hatchery fish. As one popular bumper-sticker says, "Real fish are born to be wild."

Tainting the water even further is the high cost of hatcheries. Washington's Cowlitz hatchery, for example, cost approximately $10 million (U.S.) to build. At that kind of price level, every salmon that is hatched, makes it to adulthood and returns to

To Save the Salmon

spawn has cost a great deal of money. Each adult chinook that returns to Oregon's Grande Ronde hatchery costs over $875 (U.S.) to produce. Each spring chinook that returns to the Columbia River's Irrigon hatchery costs an incredible $10,000 (U.S.) to produce.

However, hatcheries do have a role to play in breeding threatened species of salmon and in stocking streams where no wild stocks of salmon occur. Some excellent angling opportunities now exist only because of the progeny of hatcheries.

SPAWNING CHANNELS

Because of the limited area within hatcheries and the high cost of building such facilities, spawning channels have gained favor as an artificial means of rearing salmon. The idea originated in Europe, where spawning channels were used as early as 1765.

A spawning channel is a shallow, man-made channel with a gravel bottom and sides built of gravel, rock or concrete. The gravel at the bottom of the channel is carefully chosen to match the preference of the species being cultivated, and the flow of water over the gravel is carefully controlled to keep the eggs at the optimum temperature.

When the eggs hatch, the alevins stay in the channels for a short time and then migrate to adjacent lakes or rivers. The channels are usually fenced to keep out four-legged predators and are often covered with nets to deter kingfishers, owls, hawks, eagles and ospreys.

Spawning channels can dramatically improve the egg-to-fry survival rate. For chum salmon, for example, only 9 percent of the eggs survive to the fry stage in the wild. In a spawning channel, this rate is improved to 60 to 70 percent. That difference can mean millions of fish, at a relatively low cost.

STREAM ENHANCEMENT

All across North America, local efforts are under way to erase the damage that humans have done to fish-bearing streams. Many communities have annual events where debris is hauled out of streams and blockages to fish migration are removed.

Shade trees can be planted along rivers to cool the waters, and pools can be dug to provide spots where fish can rest and hide from predators. Streambank erosion can be reduced by placing stones or concrete as "rip-rap" that softens the erosive force of water. Even the simple act of erecting fences to keep out livestock can go a long way toward conserving a salmon stream.

In Snohomish County, Washington, the public works department has sponsored adopt-a-stream projects for community groups with great success. Groups have hatched salmon eggs, replanted streambanks and removed stream debris using donated money and volunteer muscle. The big winners have been the salmon.

FISH LADDERS

The greatest salmon river in North America is the Fraser River, which has its headwaters high in the snow-frosted peaks of central British Columbia and flows into the sea at Vancouver. By far the most dangerous portion of the river to fish is Hell's Gate, a canyon located 32 miles (51 km) north of the city of Hope. There the canyon walls are only 110 feet (34 m) wide, and the roar of the river does indeed conjure an aural image of the gates of Hell. Water rushes through Hell's Gate at the rate of 20 feet (6 m) per second, overwhelming all but the strongest of salmon.

In 1911 and 1912, railroad builders blasted tons of rock along Hell's Gate, and much of the debris fell into this precious river. In 1914, a single slide on the east side of the river filled almost half of the channel. The 1913 commercial catch of sockeyes on the Fraser was 31 million fish, a record that has never been surpassed. The catch after the disasters of 1911, 1912 and 1914 decreased by 84 percent. The Fraser River's salmon population appeared to be doomed.

At the University of Washington, engineers made a concrete model of the canyon and studied the tortuous path the fish had to take to make it upstream. Construction began in 1944 of two huge concrete runways, one on each side of the canyon, containing a series of obstacles 18 feet (5.5 m) apart that slow the water to one-sixteenth its normal speed and theoretically provide the fish with an easy path upstream. The baffles also create a long series of pools separating steps 10 inches (25 cm) in height, so that salmon can jump up to each pool, rest and continue on until they are out of the flume.

These fish ladders were some of the first used in North America and were long pointed to with pride as the epitome of salmon conservation. However, Scott Hinch of the University of British Columbia's Westwater Research Centre recently found that the Hell's Gate fishway is very inefficient. The average fish takes three days to find its way through the fishway. Of 20 sockeye tracked by Hinch in 1993, not one made it through the canyon.

Modern fish ladders are a bit more efficient, but that efficiency comes at a high price. Alaska's Paint River ladder, built in 1991, cost $2.7 million (U.S.).

Still, where natural obstructions such as waterfalls or man-made blockages prevent salmon from getting upstream to their spawning grounds, fish ladders are one way that biologists can give the fish a helping hand.

Alternatives to ladders include, among other things, such ideas as concrete runways and the actual transport of salmon downstream. At the Little Goose Dam on the Lower Snake River in Washington, a 2,000-foot (609-m)-long runway collects fish and carries them past the dam.

Farther along the Snake River, at the Lower Granite Dam, salmon are collected from the river each spring, and daily barges take about 250,000 chinook smolts from Idaho past the dangerous dams to a release spot downstream in Washington.

These alternatives underline the high value that people put on salmon; there are very few other species for which humans will go to such ends. Such is the value of the King of the Pacific.

RESTOCKING

Long ago, Native people carried fish in bark baskets to remote lakes in attempts to build new stocks. The techniques were primitive, but the idea was sound.

Today, helicopters have replaced the bark baskets as biologists attempt to start new salmon stocks or rebuild dwindling populations.

Restocking tends to have mixed results, as the fish used are primarily hatchery fish and many do not return to spawn. Nor can fish from other stocks be used, for nine times out of ten they will only return to the streams of their birth.

The other major problem with the technique is cost: helicopter time does not come cheap, and all too many fisheries departments now operate on ever-dwindling budgets.

LAKE FERTILIZATION

In lakes where high precipitation causes high runoff, thus depleting the lake of its nutrients, artificial fertilization can replenish the lake and boost salmon populations.

The best-known example of lake fertilization is Vancouver Island's Great Central Lake, where huge amounts of fertilizer were released into the lake in a program that began in 1970. The nutrients were dropped into the lake at weekly intervals by boat, and the results were impressive. The fertilization resulted in an eightfold increase in the abundance of zooplankton, and a doubling in the growth rate of sockeye fry. Over the long term, biologists boasted a twentyfold increase in the number of sockeye adults that returned to the lake for spawning. Other lakes are now being fertilized as well, primarily by aerial spraying. The prohibitive factor, once again, is cost.

FISH FARMS

Inevitably, the decline of wild salmon stocks has boosted the economic attractiveness of fish farming, or aquaculture. In many spots along the Pacific Coast, nylon and wire pens are used to hold juvenile salmon in one place, where they can then be fattened up before harvesting. Coho and chinook are especially popular choices for fish farms, due to their large size.

Like any form of farming, fish farming is not without its hazards. In secluded bays, fish waste can then build up on the sea bottom and pollute the water. Algae blooms may also develop if the waste really piles up. The cost of transporting the salmon to market can be high. Stormy weather can destroy pens and allow the escape of fish, causing fears about competition with wild salmon for food and potential interbreeding.

Despite the many drawbacks of fish farms, the highest-priced freshwater fish in North America is the salmon, and the market

To Save the Salmon

right now for this fish is strong. Almost a third of the salmon consumed in North America now originates on fish farms. According to Rebecca J. Goldburg, a biologist with the Environmental Defense Fund, "aquaculture is now the fastest-growing segment of the U.S. agriculture industry."[2] Worldwide, consumption of farm-raised salmon now exceeds that of wild salmon.

Unfortunately, all of these conservation techniques have not come cheap. On the Columbia River alone, over $1 billion has been spent on hatcheries, ladders, river enhancement and other conservation techniques. Izaac Walton would be amazed.

7 · A HISTORY OF SALMON FISHING IN NORTH AMERICA

"It is a wonder that there are so many fish with the little protection that they have had."

WILLIAM BARKER, CANNER, EARLY 1900S

Over the past century and a half, the exploitation of the salmon resource in North America has had an eerie parallel to the exploitation of the forest resource. The early use of fish traps and huge gillnets had the same result on the fishery as early clearcutting did on the forests. And with both industries, only in the past few decades has the concept of "sustainable development" even been considered.

But unlike a grove of trees, which may take 100 or 200 years to regrow, the salmon has a short life cycle, which allows it potentially to turn around drastic declines within a few years—if managed properly.

What is most remarkable about the following history of salmon fishing in North America is the sheer number of warnings over the past hundred years about the sad state of the salmon fishery—and the fact that, sadly, all of them have been ignored.

And what is most tragic is that Canada has followed in the footsteps of the United States by failing to acknowledge the seriousness of the salmon situation, until it is almost too late.

THE EARLY YEARS: 1830–1915

The first commercial use of salmon in North America came when the Hudson's Bay Company obtained salmon in trade from local Native peoples. At first, this salmon was used as food for those working at the fur-trading posts. Around 1830, however, the Bay began to barrel salt-cured salmon for export, sending the barrels to markets as far away as Hawaii and Asia. By 1847, profits from the sale of salmon exceeded those from the sale of furs. There was, however, one big problem: by the time the fish got to their distant destinations, the wooden barrels had often rotted and the salmon inside had done the same.

The solution came from an unlikely source: Napoleon Bonaparte. The famed army commander couldn't keep food for his armies fresh, so he held a contest, with a prize of 1,200 French francs to go to the first person who could invent a method of food preservation. The winner was Nicolas Appert, a winemaker and chef, who in 1809 sealed food in tin plate to solve Napoleon's food problems. This was the world's first canned food, and our eating habits haven't been the same since.

The first commercial Pacific salmon cannery in North America opened in 1864 in California, where each can was painstakingly hand-soldered. Canada's first canned Pacific salmon was first cooked over a kitchen stove and then canned in New Westminster, British Columbia, in 1867. British Columbia's first commercial cannery opened in 1871. The 1-pound (0.5-kg) cans of salmon sold for a mere ten cents each.

Canneries spread quickly throughout the Pacific Northwest; by 1874, there were a dozen in Oregon between Astoria and Portland. Alaska's first canneries opened in 1878, in Klawock and Sitka. By 1883, there were fifty-five canneries on or near the Columbia River, between Oregon and Washington.

Meanwhile, in California, gold had been discovered in 1848 and hydraulic mining had begun on the salmon-rich Sacramento River in 1853. Much of the mining waste was simply dumped into the river, and salmon runs began a slow and steady decline.

Around 1864, approximately ten years later, gillnets began to be used for the first time on the Columbia and Fraser River salmon fisheries. In the beginning there were no regulations regarding their use, and huge nets stretched almost completely across portions of the rivers, often extending right to the rivers' beds. Whole salmon runs could thus be trapped and collected. It was not until 1871 that the state of Washington enacted the first regulations making it illegal to place any kind of weirs or nets across more than two-thirds of a fish-bearing stream or river. In 1878 and 1879, Oregon and Washington both enacted laws governing the minimum mesh sizes for weirs and nets.

North of the border, Canada's Constitution Act of 1867 gave jurisdiction over the "seacoast and inland fisheries" to the new Dominion government. For the next century and a half, Canadian politicians and fishers argued fiercely over the management of the West Coast fishery by Easterners. It was not until 1936, however, that a federal Minister of Fisheries even visited the Pacific coast. And it was not until many decades later that a Westerner held that crucial position.

In 1868, the Fisheries Act created Canada's Department of Marine and Fisheries, now known as the Department of Fisheries and Oceans (DFO). The first federal fisheries agent for British Columbia wasn't appointed until 1875. Most early fisheries departments were sadly understaffed, with far too few boats and employees. For example, as late as 1882, there were only two fishery officers patrolling the entire British Columbia coast.

But as canneries spread across the Pacific Northwest, the demand for fish and fisheries officers skyrocketed. Ironically, the first canned salmon exports went to the United Kingdom, whose own salmon streams had already been destroyed as a result of pollution from the Industrial Revolution.

The first commercial fishing licenses in British Columbia were issued in 1877, primarily to canners, who controlled the bulk of the fishing fleet.

In that same year, the state of Washington began to set aside seasons and weekends that were closed to fishing, two basic concepts of fish management. Oregon followed suit in 1878.

One of the most unusual pieces of early salmon-catching equipment was the fish wheel, a mini–Ferris wheel that scooped fish right out of the water. Fish wheels were first used on the Columbia River in 1879, where on a single day in 1913 an amazing 70,000

A History of Salmon Fishing in North America

pounds (32,000 kg) of salmon were caught. Fish wheels were banned in Oregon in 1926 and in Washington in 1934.

Another popular piece of equipment was the purse seine. The use of purse seines, at first illegal in British Columbia due to their wholesale catching technique, spread quickly throughout the province. In 1884, there were only 117 seines in use. Sixteen years later, there were more than 1,000.

The increasing efficiency of the fishing fleet meant that canneries often could not keep up with the number of fish brought to them. In 1877, 5,000 dead fish were thrown back in a single day because there were no facilities to hand for preserving them. An ensuing investigation found that one cannery alone had discarded as many as 3,000 fish in one day.

In the early days of the fishery, no one considered that the resource could be overexploited. But in the United States, salmon fishers were already seeing sharp declines in their catches. The peak canned salmon output from the Columbia River was in 1883. After that date, it steadily declined.

Fish traps were developed in 1885, and were commonplace in Puget Sound and the Strait of Juan de Fuca, taking advantage of the salmon's migration route south of Vancouver Island through American waters. Thus began the first fight over fish that shared both Canadian and U.S. waters.

To construct a fish trap, a nearshore barricade more than 2,000 feet (600 m) long was attached to piles, funneling fish into a small area, from which they could then be dip-netted out. One such trap was documented to have caught 75,000 fish in one day. In one year, it was estimated that 60 percent of the Fraser River run had been taken in fish traps. By the late 1920s, over 400 fish traps were in use in northwestern rivers in the United States.

Unlike gillnets, which at least allow the escape of small fish, fish traps catch everything. They were banned in B.C. waters in 1900. Their continued use in American waters was a bone of contention for many years.

At first, commercial salmon fishers sought only the red flesh of chinooks and sockeyes, and all other fish were discarded as garbage. There were no laws regarding the disposal of fish wastes, and river banks were lined with rotting fish.

Conditions along the Fraser River were so bad that, in 1887, an outbreak of typhoid fever was blamed on the unsanitary conditions around the canneries. It was estimated that over 9 million pounds (4 million kg) of rotting salmon were dumped on the Fraser River each year. From Garry Point, at the mouth of the Fraser River, for several miles inland, a layer of decomposing salmon 24 inches (60 cm) deep and 200 feet (60 m) across littered the shore.

In 1888, Frances Fuller Victor wrote passionately that "Nature does not provide against such greed...there is a prospect that the salmon, like the buffalo, may become extinct."[1] That same year, the Victoria Board of Trade recommended that a license scheme be enacted to limit fishing efforts on the Fraser River.

And so it was that, in 1889, the first Canadian federal fishing regulations appeared. A license requirement to net for salmon was established, with restrictions on net size and type; gillnets were limited to a depth of 900 feet (274 m) and to one-third of the river's width; a weekend closed season was set; and the use of explosives, which had been regularly used in Burrard Inlet until then, was disallowed.

Even after the establishment of the new fishing regulations, overfishing remained commonplace. On one single day in the early 1890s, two fishers in one single skiff took 1,100 salmon.

It wasn't until 1892 that regulations on the disposal of fish refuse were finally established. That same year, yet another warning regarding overfishing came when Chief Charlie Caplin of the Musqueam warned that "the nets are too long... [and have] a tendency to kill them all.... It will destroy the salmon in time."[2]

By that same year, the output from Alaskan canneries exceeded that from California, Oregon and Washington for the first time as more and more fishers plied the rich frigid waters off the coast of Alaska.

In 1893, more voices added to the din demanding a reduction in the salmon catch. R.D. Hume, a pioneer American canner, wrote that, "unless...steps are taken, in less than ten years, the packing of salmon on the Columbia River will have become impossible as a business proposition."[3]

Later that same year, the entire adult population of Ladner's Landing, British Columbia, signed a petition to protest the dumping of unwanted fish remains from the canneries. These canneries were flagrantly ignoring the new fish-disposal regulations.

The next year, 1894, saw even more warnings regarding the declining numbers of salmon. Hollister D. McGuire, Oregon Fish and Game Protector, wrote passionately, "it is only a matter of a few years under present conditions when the Chinooks of the Columbia will be as scarce as the beaver that was once so plentiful in our streams."[4] In fact, the peak catch of chinook from the Columbia had already occurred, in 1883, and was already steadily declining when McGuire wrote those words.

In light of the widespread overfishing, it seems tragic that great efforts were made to penalize just the Native fishery. In 1894, new regulations in Canada outlawed fish weirs and other traditional Native technologies, including traps and pens. Gaffs, spears and foul-hooks were prohibited in Oregon in 1901.

In 1894, the U.S. Fish Commission reported that placer mining on the upper Boise River had seriously harmed the salmon runs, echoing problems seen in California forty years earlier.

By 1895, there were still few regulations governing the size of nets on the Columbia River. Some of the gillnets used stretched over 1,800 feet (550 m) long, leaving little room for some fish to escape in order to spawn and continue the stocks.

In 1896, floating fish traps were tried for the first time, off Alaska's Kodiak Island, with disappointing results as the rocky seas reduced them to firewood in a mere matter of weeks.

During the huge 1897 Fraser River sockeye run, many fishers overcaught their limit and simply dumped the unwanted fish overboard. So many fish were caught, in fact, that for the first time in Canadian history the canners canned over a million cases of salmon.

In 1898, a dam was built across the Quesnel River in central British Columbia to store water for a gold-mining operation nearby. Unable to bypass the dam, the Quesnel River sockeye run slowly began to die off, dwindling from 15 million fish to just over 1,000. The dam was not removed for twenty-three years. Other gold-mining operations in the Cariboo District dumped mine wastes into the Horsefly and Quesnel Rivers and diverted their waters, destroying the habitat of thousands of salmon.

And so, by the turn of the century, overfishing, pollution and disregard for regulations had already seriously damaged many salmon stocks. For three-quarters of the next century, there was little improvement.

One of the major hallmarks of the twentieth century was a huge leap forward in the rate of technology development. The fishing business was no exception. Trollers went into commercial use in British Columbia around the year 1899. In the early years of the B.C. fishery, trollers required no license whatsoever. Trollers did not come into common use in Oregon until about 1912.

In 1901, a record Canadian pack of 2 million cases of salmon had canners laughing all the way to the bank. But only three years later, that pack had shrunk to 196,107 cases and it was obvious that the salmon fishery was in big trouble.

A California biologist named John P. Babcock was brought in as Fisheries Commissioner for British Columbia to reverse the decline of the salmon fishery. His first project, the Seton Lake hatchery, was a dismal failure. Babcock didn't believe the scientific findings about the specificity of genetic stocks, and used 40 million salmon eggs collected from a number of different sources to start the hatchery. As a result, almost no fish returned to spawn.

Many in the salmon business were slow to accept the new idea of salmon stocks being unique to certain streams. In 1883, Livingstone Stone, an agent of the U.S. Fish Commission, wrote that he believed the salmon ran up rivers randomly, attracted best by "a strong, rapid current of cold water."[5] In Oregon, the futile practice of transferring salmon eggs from hatcheries in one area to release sites in long-distant streams persisted until 1921.

Technical developments continued throughout the early 1900s. The first commercial salmon-freezing units appeared at about 1902. This invention allowed more fish to be caught and preserved. Coho and chinook, which were mostly caught by trolling, were the main species frozen.

By 1903, one of the earliest fishing unions, the Fishermen's Protective Union of the Pacific Coast and Alaska, had attracted more than 3,000 members.

That same year, widespread concern about mismanagement of the salmon fishery in Canada led to the first fisheries commission, a toothless and weak exercise that produced no concrete results.

Two years later, Commissioner Babcock recommended the closure of fishing traps in the state of Washington. The state government ignored his recommendation.

In 1905, the spinning reel was invented in England and its use quickly spread to North America, heralding the modern era of sports fishing.

Three years later, provincial legislation that aimed to take over the management of B.C. fishing was overturned by Ottawa, and the cry over absentee management of the fishing resource reached a fever pitch.

In 1908, Canada called for an international treaty to regulate the American–Canadian joint salmon stocks. After massive lobbying by fishers from Washington state, the idea failed to pass in U.S. Congress.

The only two pieces of good news in 1908, as far as salmon were concerned, were the opening of the Pacific Biological Station in Nanaimo, which has conducted valuable research on salmon ever since, and the prohibiting of salmon fishing in the narrows of the upper Columbia River, where overfishing was rampant.

One of the worst salmon-related disasters of 1908 came when a logging company built a splash dam across the Upper Adams River to flush logs downstream, nearly destroying the Upper Adams sockeye run completely. Unbelievably, the dam was not removed until 1945.

In 1910, responding to declining salmon numbers, the state government of California prohibited commercial salmon fishing in the Rogue River and its tributaries.

Although the word "pollution" had not yet become part of everyday vocabulary, its tragic effects spread across the land in the early part of this century. The Oregon Fish and Game Commission was aware that the situation was hurting fish, stating that "dumping the sewage of cities, the waste of mills and factories and filth of all kinds into our public waters...will completely deplete our streams of fish, if it is allowed to continue."[6] But they did little to stop it.

That same year, 1911, was a landmark for another reason: it marked the date of the highest total catch of salmon from the Columbia River in modern times; from then on the catch steadily

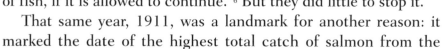

declined, a tragic end to what had been a huge resource.

In 1912, gasoline engines began to appear in the salmon fishery, raising old boats to a new level of efficiency. The year 1912 also saw the birth of the Deep Sea Fishermen's Union of the Pacific, another early attempt at giving fishers united bargaining power.

In 1913–14, what has been called the "greatest single environ-mental disaster in the province's history" occurred when sloppy railroad construction techniques by the Canadian Northern Railway and the Canadian Pacific Railway along the banks of B.C.'s Fraser River caused huge landslides into Hell's Canyon, a narrow upstream portion of the river. Hundreds of thousands of fish were unable to make it further upstream and died on the spot.

Unbelievably, federal Fisheries inspector F.H. Cunningham made things even worse when he allowed fishers to continue tak-ing migrating fish out of the river. Ottawa overruled him and ordered an immediate closure of the Fraser River fishery, but Cunningham ignored these instructions. Many of the surviving salmon were then snapped up by greedy fishers, decreasing even further the number of fish that made it upstream to spawn.

One side effect of the landslides was that, due to the drastic shortage of sockeye salmon after the disaster, pinks and chums were added to the market and were surprisingly well accepted by consumers, thus beginning yet another round of depleting a thus-far-untouched species.

No charges were ever laid against the railroad companies for the massive destruction they caused.

THE BOOM YEARS: 1916–1945

In 1917, the rich Puget Sound fishery in northern Washington reached its peak and began a slow decline.

The next year, the progression of power winches to reel in fish-ing lines modernized the trolling industry and the west-coast salmon catch increased yet again. By 1919, there were between 1,000 and 2,000 trollers working off the mouth of the Columbia River alone.

In Canada, a second major commission on the west-coast fish-ery was called in 1922, with few results.

It is an axiom of history that, after a world war, there is a boom in industry as new technologies are adapted for civilian use and as manpower returns to the workforce. This held true for the fishing industry after the First World War.

In Canada, purse seining tripled in popularity, from 142 boats in 1922 to 406 boats only four years later. In 1923, Assistant Minister of Fisheries William A. Found was forced to ban any form of seining within 1,200 feet (366 m) of a creek or river mouth. He also recommended hiring sufficient Fisheries officers to prevent illegal fishing, a wise suggestion that Ottawa ignored.

Many men returning from the war went into logging, and many pristine streams throughout the Pacific Northwest suffered the consequences. As early as 1919, legislation to protect the streams was enacted, when the Oregon legislature wisely banned the driving of free logs down rivers and streams.

By the late 1920s, diesel engines were in common use, permitting the use of larger boats. And larger boats caught yet more fish.

In 1924, the DFO began the first intensive study of the salmon life cycle in Canada and began a program of salmonid enhancement, primarily through the use of hatcheries.

But there is little use in adding more fish to the fishery if the fishery itself is not managed properly. Frustrated by a lack of interest from Ottawa, in 1928, B.C. canners set up their own regulations to manage the fishery. They divided the coast into seventeen areas, set strict limits on the numbers of fishers allowed to operate in each area, and reduced the number of licenses. These moves are widely accepted as marking the start of modern salmon management in Canada.

They were followed in 1932 by an important new clause to the Canadian Fisheries Act, which stated that "no person engaging in logging, lumbering, land clearing or other operations, shall put or knowingly permit to be put, any slash, stumps or other debris into any water frequented by fish."[7]

Other developments had strong impacts on the salmon fishery. In the 1930s, flash-freezing was invented, increasing the demand for coho and chinook. During this same decade, the town of Ketchikan, Alaska, became the world's leading producer of canned salmon.

Portable chainsaws were developed in 1933, heralding the start

of extensive logging operations at a time when few regulations
existed to protect salmon streams.

That same year also saw the completion of the Rock Island
Dam, the first of the great dams that blocked fish migration on the
Columbia River.

In 1934, the government of the state of Washington moved to
eliminate fixed gear on their side of the Columbia River, by out-
lawing fish wheels, traps, seines and set nets.

In 1937, the International Pacific Salmon Fisheries Commission was created, headquartered in New Westminster, British
Columbia. Its initial mission was to protect the Fraser River sockeye stocks, which brought in the most money for the canners. A
secondary goal was to fairly apportion harvests between U.S. and
B.C. fishers. Although the commission did a good job with its initial mission, it failed miserably with its secondary goal.

That same year, fears were officially raised about the future of
the Columbia River salmon when U.S. Commissioner of Fisheries
Frank Bell admitted that "the development of the Columbia River
for power and agriculture imperils an ancient industry, the salmon
fisheries."[8]

Bell's fears were reflected in 1938 with the passing of the
Mitchell Act, which funded measures to preserve and protect the
Columbia River salmon, including hatcheries, fish ladders and
habitat-restoration projects.

As a result of new technology, including radio telephones, echo
sounders and diesel engines, the volume of the salmon catch in
British Columbia almost tripled between 1931 and 1940, though
few people expressed concern about the growing volume of the
catch.

Almost unheralded at the time was the creation in March 1945
of the United Fishermen and Allied Workers Union (UFAWU), a
strong voice for fishers that would get louder in years to come.

THE MODERN ERA: 1946–1989
After the Second World War, the availability of new boats and new
technology transformed the fishing industry into a highly efficient
machine, taking higher and higher percentages of the salmon
available. Many men returning from the war took advantage of the

new technology and entered the fishing business for the first time. The Butedale seine fishery in British Columbia, for example, increased from only 25 boats in the 1930s to 141 by 1948.

The late 1940s also saw a boom in recreational fishing when a large number of charter and private boats entered the recreational fleet.

In 1948, Oregon first began setting fish-size restrictions for the commercial troll fishery. Prior to that year, there were few restrictions on either size or gear.

In the fervor of postwar industrialization, the B.C. government in 1949 invited Alcan (The Aluminium Company of Canada) to build a new smelter in the province. Alcan got cheap land, and free mineral rights, and was even granted permission to build without fisheries approval. They were also told to use adjacent river systems for power generation as they saw fit. As a result of the government's generosity, the Nanika and Nechako River salmon runs were seriously harmed. In the Nechako, the chinook run decreased from several thousand fish to fewer than fifty.

But all was not doom and gloom in Canada's westernmost province. The first sizable spawning channel for salmon was built in British Columbia in 1954, and its success led to dozens of imitators across the continent.

By the 1950s, seiners had become the fishing boat of choice and had surpassed gillnetters in the poundage of salmon caught.

The 1950s also saw the development of the power block for hauling in trolling gear and the catches of salmon by trollers increased dramatically. The state of Oregon once again was at the front of the pack, with new recreational-troll-fishery regulations in 1955 that included size limits for chinook, coho and pinks.

As the catch of salmon escalated, the canneries often couldn't keep up with the numbers of fish brought to them. In 1962, thousands of whole salmon were dumped back into the rivers for this reason.

The push for industry in British Columbia led to inevitable problems with pollution. For example, in 1957, DDT was sprayed along the Keogh River on Vancouver Island to control plant growth, unintentionally reducing the salmon spawners from 20,000 to fewer than 100. A 1961 brief by the UFAWU cited their opinion that pollution was one of the two main reasons for the decline in the salmon runs (the other was overfishing on the high seas).

In the late 1950s, a consortium of power utilities proposed construction of a dam just below the confluence of the Snake and Salmon Rivers in Idaho. The Federal Power Commission licensed the project in 1964, but the Interior Secretary, Stewart Udall, filed suit to stop the dam. In 1967, Justice William O. Douglas backed Udall in an unusual action, ruling that "the destruction of anadromous fish in our western waters is so notorious that we cannot believe that Congress...authorized their ultimate demise."[9]

One dam that was completed was the controversial Dalles Dam on the lower Columbia River, finished in 1957. Waters collecting behind the dam then submerged Celilo Falls, a traditional Native fishing ground, adding gasoline to the flames of the burgeoning Native-rights movement.

In 1958, the Adams River sockeye run had the best returns since the disaster of the 1913–14 Hell's Gate slides. The number of sockeye swamped the canneries along the lower Fraser River and prompted federal fishery officials to dub the excess fish "undesirable." To get rid of the unwanted fish, they erected an electric fence at the mouth of the Adams River and electrocuted a million salmon in one of the worst instances of mismanagement to date. The result was very weak sockeye returns for many years afterward.

By 1961, the number of licensed fishers in British Columbia had grown to more than 15,000. The DFO recommended a reduction of one-third to one-half of the fleet, and a five-year moratorium on new licenses, but this sensible idea died when a new government took power in Ottawa.

In 1968, the new Liberal Fisheries Minister for Canada, Jack Davis, announced that license limitation would be his top priority. By September 1969, the fishing fleet had decreased by 571, to 6,977 boats. By 1974, an additional 361 boats left the fleet through license buybacks.

The controversy over the fleet reduction led to a 1973 study by University of British Columbia economics professor Peter Pearse. Pearse's final report recommended further fleet rationalizations,

A History of Salmon Fishing in North America

particularly stressing the need to reduce the number of gillnetters and trollers. He also recommended that the license buybacks continue.

As salmon stocks dwindled across the Pacific Northwest, a new factor appeared on the horizon: commercial fish farming. The first fish farm in Washington opened in 1969. Two years later, Crown Zellerbach, a huge Washington-based logging company, opened British Columbia's first salmon farm in Cousins Inlet near their Ocean Falls pulp mill. The company did not apply for any of the necessary permits for its operation and it was closed down by the DFO the next year. The seed had been planted, however, and fish farming became a contentious issue in the years to come, with particular concerns over fish wastes, escapees, introduced disease and interbreeding with wild stocks.

By the 1970s, there were ominous signs that the salmon fishery was in big trouble. In British Columbia, chinook stocks were decreasing in most coastal systems, coho stocks had decreased in 5 major areas, and steelhead runs were stable in only 5 of the 400 known steelhead streams.

Fortunately for salmon, the 1960s and 1970s marked a time of awakening to the state of the environment, a time when people began to care about the other inhabitants of planet Earth.

In 1971, Oregon became the first American state to pass broad forest-practices legislation aimed at protecting fish-bearing streams.

The oil crisis of the 1970s, which saw fuel costs rise up to 400 percent, put new pressures on individual fishers, and many were forced into bankruptcy as a result.

In 1974, Native-rights proponents celebrated a major victory in the United States when Washington state federal judge George Boldt ruled that non-treaty Native fishers were entitled to up to 50 percent of the salmon harvest in that state. Five years later, Supreme Court Justice John Paul Stevens upheld the controversial *Boldt* decision, writing that the "resource has now become scarce, and the meaning of the Indians' treaty right to take fish has accordingly become critical."[10]

In 1976, the U.S. Magnuson Fishery Conservation and Management Act required fish managers to achieve the "maximum sustainable yield and optimum yield from the fishery,"[11] blurry terms which have been argued over ever since. In that same year, the U.S. exclusive fishing zone was extended to 200 miles (300 km) offshore, effectively protecting the inshore fisheries from foreign fishers. Canada similarly extended its offshore jurisdiction the following year.

Public pressure in the 1970s finally forced the Canadian federal government to hold a series of public hearings on the management of the salmon fishery.

The government learned from these hearings that Canadians favored a salmon-enhancement program that would restore the fish before the situation worsened. As a result, in 1977 federal Fisheries minister Romeo LeBlanc announced that the government was committing $150 million over the next five years as the first phase of a new Salmonid Enhancement Program.

By 1981, only $47 million had been spent—only half that had been promised—mostly for costly fish hatcheries, in seeming defiance of the public's demand for habitat restoration and natural production of wild fish.

The public also grew tired of the lack of enforcement of regulations pertaining to salmon. In 1977, amendments to the Fisheries Act made it illegal to pollute or contaminate fish habitat, but officials were slow to enforce the regulations for fear of scaring off big business.

The lack of action on the part of the DFO also came at a bad time for the salmon. By 1980, 70 percent of the Fraser River watershed wetlands had been destroyed and all the remaining salmon habitat had become precious.

In 1980, U.S. Congress passed the Northwest Power Act, which made fish and wildlife "a co-equal partner with other uses"[12] of the Columbia River, a huge victory for American environmentalists.

Peter Pearse took charge in 1980 of yet another inquiry into the Canadian fishing industry. His inquiry, the most comprehensive ever, led to the Common Pacific Fisheries Policy report of 1983, which recommended a massive license buyback program that aimed to reduce overfishing. More than 4,000 fishing boats remained in the fleet at this time.

In 1981, the DFO again came under fire when it allowed Amax

Corporation to dump toxic mine waste into the ocean in quantities almost 80,000 times higher than those allowed under the Fisheries Act.

The new federal Fisheries Minister of Canada, Pierre de Bané, followed the Pearse recommendations in 1984 when he unveiled the Pacific Fisheries Restructuring Act. This act would have reduced the fishing fleet by 45 percent and would have introduced widespread fishery closures in order to allow salmon stocks to build up. Although it was endorsed by Peter Pearse and other qualified authorities, the bill was defeated in Ottawa.

Soon after, the Mulroney Conservative government swept into power, strongly backed by big business. John Fraser, a B.C. resident, became Fisheries minister. He vowed to establish a $100-million license-buyback program and to create a strong second phase of the Salmonid Enhancement Program, but soon backed down after heavy lobbying by fishers. The second phase was put on hold, the Salmonid Enhancement Program staff were cut by a third, and the buyback scheme was canceled. Fraser was replaced by Eric Nielsen, and the new Fisheries minister's first act was to cancel the second phase of the Salmonid Enhancement Program. This critical blow couldn't have come at a worse time for the dwindling salmon stocks.

After over a decade of heated negotiations, the United States and Canada signed a draft Interception Treaty in 1982, aimed at solving the problem of fishers in one legal jurisdiction intercepting salmon spawned in another jurisdiction. The treaty was directed at Fraser River stocks, which are regularly intercepted by Alaskan fishers, and Columbia River stocks, which are often taken by Canadian fishers. However, the treaty failed to receive ratification following loud objections by Alaskan fishers.

Better success was achieved with the Columbia Basin Fish and Wildlife Program, enacted in 1982, and aimed at restoring fish and wildlife populations harmed by hydro dam developments throughout the Columbia River basin. The program is still active today.

That same year, Oregon state began requiring that barbless hooks be used in some areas by recreational ocean fishers, a foresighted measure that allows more successful catch-and-release fishing.

Despite its rocky start in the 1970s, fish farming took off in British Columbia in the 1980s, backed by millions of dollars of support from the government. The DFO gave 35 million coho and chinook eggs to fish farms, amid a scream of protest from both environmentalists and fishers. Geoff Meggs, spokesman for the United Fishermen and Allied Workers Union, loudly criticized the DFO for providing fish farms with salmon eggs intended to help the wild fishery stocks.

To make matters worse, many of the fish farmed were Atlantic salmon, which are less aggressive than other salmon species, and thus more suitable for farming in crowded pens. They also grow more quickly in these pens.

DEATH OF THE FISHERY: 1990 TO DATE

Salmon populations in the lower forty-eight states continued to plummet throughout the late 1980s. As a result, the U.S. National Marine Fisheries Service was petitioned in 1990 by a number of special-interest groups to list various salmon stocks under the Endangered Species Act (ESA). In 1991, the Snake River sockeye was listed as endangered, the first American salmon to be so listed. Today, both the lower California steelhead and the Sacramento River winter-run chinooks are listed as endangered, and a number of Snake River chinook stocks are on the threatened list.

The ESA proceedings stirred up great public interest, with a "Salmon Summit" held in 1990 for interested parties to discuss the decline of the salmon in the Pacific Northwest.

In 1991, the North Pacific Anadromous Stocks Convention, signed by Canada and the other North Pacific nations, aimed at coordinating efforts at salmon conservation and research.

March 1991 saw a landmark article entitled "Pacific Salmon at the Crossroads" in *Fisheries*, the official journal of the American Fisheries Society. In the article, noted biologists listed 214 U.S. salmon stocks that had been depleted. Of the 214, 106 were already extinct, 101 were considered to be at high risk of extinction, 58 at moderate risk, and 54 of special concern. About one in three of the depleted stocks were from the Columbia or Snake River systems.

While the salmon picture in the lower forty-eight states was getting rather dim, it was still bright in Alaska. The 1991 recreational and commercial catch of pinks in Alaska hit an incredible 128,487,316 fish.

That same year, a 5-pound (2-kg) male Atlantic salmon was discovered attempting to spawn with a cutthroat trout in Roberts Creek, British Columbia. This was the first documented instance of an escaped Atlantic salmon attempting to spawn in B.C. waters, something that fish farmers said could never happen. (Escaped Atlantic salmon can be recognized by their large scales, large black dots on their back, lack of spots on their tail, eight to eleven anal fin rays, and large black spots on their gill cover. In addition, they may have noticeably eroded fins from captivity in pens.) Conservationists were outraged, and some fishers tried to redirect the resulting attention elsewhere.

By the early 1990s, commercial fishers were engaged in strong lobbies aimed at reducing the take of salmon by aboriginal peoples. One media campaign in 1992 blamed "massive Native poaching" as the cause of destroyed sockeye runs. This in spite of the fact that the Native fishery accounted only for 5 percent of the total catch.

Between 1991 and 1994, more than 100,000 Atlantic salmon escaped from B.C. fish farms, but, since reporting is voluntary, the actual number is thought to have been much higher. In 1993, 21 Atlantic salmon were sighted in rivers and streams along the coast, igniting new fears about exotic fish spawning in B.C. waters. The next year, 31 Atlantic salmon were similarly sighted; all were sexually mature and capable of spawning.

Soon after these sightings, it was discovered that farmed Atlantic salmon in Norway had escaped into streams and successfully spawned. Although many biologists think interbreeding between Atlantic and Pacific salmon is unlikely, research at DFO's West Vancouver laboratory found that it *is* possible. Experiments by Dr. Robert H. Devlin determined that hybrids of female Atlantic salmon and male Pacific pinks produced offspring, 5 percent of which were viable.

The year 1993 saw record runs of sockeye all along the west coast. In Alaska, the 1993 commercial and recreational catch totalled 64,597,661 sockeye. In British Columbia, 18,110,008 sockeye were caught, making up to some degree for the decline of the coho and the chinook in the years prior to this.

In 1994, however, another instance of overfishing almost destroyed the entire Adams River sockeye run. Once the run ended, it was found that the number of fish that actually reached the spawning gravels was the lowest since 1938. A public review board determined that the cause was the overfishing of sockeye in Johnstone Strait, stating that one more twelve-hour period of fishing might have completely eliminated the late run of sockeye in the Adams River.

Balancing this disaster was the fact that mounting public pressure in 1994 finally did stop Alcan's Kemano Completion Project (the final phase of hydro development for the smelter), following years of favored treatment from the provincial government. That same year, a massive international effort succeeded in clearing the north Pacific Ocean of the vast drift-net fisheries that were responsible for killing thousands of by-caught species every year.

In early 1994, U.S. president Bill Clinton finally acknowledged the effects of the declining salmon catches on west-coast communities. Upon his recommendation, the Federal Emergency Management Agency offered relief for loss of income to residents of Clatsop, Columbia, Coos, Douglas, Lane, Lincoln and Tillamook Counties in Oregon; plus Clallam, Grays Harbor, Jefferson, Pacific and Wahkiakum Counties in Washington state.

The year 1994 was also a breakthrough year for the environmental movement. After years of lobbying, both the provincial and the federal governments in Canada finally woke up to the fact that a number of salmon habitats in British Columbia were in sad shape, and a series of habitat-improvement programs were announced, one after the other. These included the Watershed Restoration Program, the B.C. Salmon Habitat Conservation Plan, the Urban Salmon Habitat Program, the Habitat Conservation Trust Fund, and the Fisheries Renewal B.C. Act.

In 1994, most of the ocean coho fishing was prohibited in Oregon, since coho stocks in the lower forty-eight states had declined to dangerously low levels.

The next year, B.C.'s Forest Practises Code established no-

A History of Salmon Fishing in North America

logging zones of 100 feet (30 m) beside salmon-bearing streams, a minimal figure that is only a third of the no-logging zone beside American streams. Craig Orr, president of the Steelhead Society of British Columbia, called the code standards "shameful."[13] The B.C. government admitted that the standards were "a compromise between biological and economic considerations."[14]

In September 1995, Fraser River gillnetters waged a loud media campaign against the Native fisheries on the Fraser River. To protest the wave of environmental protection policies that were cutting into their livelihood, about 200 gillnetters towed a gillnet boat through downtown Vancouver, broke into DFO offices, and illegally occupied them until they were finally escorted out by police.

That same year a U.S. federal court ordered a curtailment of ocean salmon fishing off the Alaskan coast due to seriously declining coho and chinook numbers.

The World Wildlife Fund also entered into the salmon fray in 1995, with recommendations for changes in the Strait of Georgia chinook salmon fishery. However, strong lobbying on the part of sport fishers kept the fishery open all season and as a result chinook catches dwindled to a record low.

In 1996, a record catch of 21,272,091 chum occurred in Alaska, pushing down chum prices so significantly that commercial fishers ended up throwing thousands of chum away as garbage, to the dismay of conservationists everywhere.

While government efforts escalated to restore damaged salmon habitat, serious problems remained in the salmon fishery itself. In 1996, the Steelhead Society of British Columbia used documents obtained from freedom of information requests to claim that fishers in northern British Columbia were consistently lying about the size of their steelhead catches. The society claimed that only 13 to 30 percent of the accidental gillnet catch of steelhead was actually reported. This meant that thousands of catches went unreported each year.

In March 1996, Canadian Fisheries minister Fred J. Mifflin announced the new Pacific Salmon Revitalization Plan, widely redubbed the Mifflin Plan. The plan intended to reduce the size of the commercial salmon fleet by 50 percent over the subsequent three years, and also set aside $80 million to buy back salmon fishing licenses (this goal was never reached, however, for by March 1999 the fleet reduction was less than 38 percent).

Later in 1996, the Canadian government asked Alaska to restrict its catch of chinook to 60,000 fish, in an effort to save the declining stocks. Sadly, Alaska ignored the request and set the limit at 155,000 fish. Frustrated Canadian fishers then prevented an Alaskan state ferry from leaving the Prince Rupert dock in an effort to protest what they deemed to be Alaskan overfishing.

Once the catch statistics for 1996 were tallied, the decline of the B.C. salmon fishery became obvious. Both the chinook and coho catches were the lowest on record.

In April 1997, the United States enacted a ban on all commercial coho fishing along the coast from California to Washington. Many conservationists recommended that Canada follow suit immediately, but once again the DFO dragged its heels for over a year.

In Alaska, the plentiful sockeye finally began to show signs of decline, with the 1997 sockeye catch one-half that of just two years earlier. The 1997 Alaskan coho catch was the lowest in over a dozen years.

The year 1998 got off to a rocky start when a U.S. judge dismissed a $325-million B.C. lawsuit alleging that Americans were taking too many Canadian-bound Pacific salmon.

In May 1998, the DFO finally closed the commercial catch of coho in Canada, to the roar of dissatisfied fishers who felt they had been unfairly picked upon.

Also that month, the Pacific Stock Assessment Review Committee slammed Canada for its management of fish habitat, stating that far too little had been done.

One month later, the DFO surprised everyone with a massive $400-million plan to aid the salmon fishery.

The sum included approximately $200 million for fishing license buybacks and incentives to modify gear for selective fishing in order to reduce the accidental by-catch of coho. According to the DFO, the number of licensed fishing boats in 1996 was over 6,000. By 1998, this figure had been halved, to about 3,000. The department expressed its wish to reduce this figure even further, by approximately 900 to 1,500 licenses. The plan also promised approximately $100 million toward salmon-habitat restoration, approximately $100 million in aid to unemployed fishers and fishing communities, and $2 million in promotion dollars toward the B.C. sports fishery.

A few days after the announcement of the aid plan, the DFO closed vast swaths of the B.C. coast to commercial salmon fishing, including the west coast of Vancouver Island, the Juan de Fuca Strait, and the rich fishing grounds north of the Queen Charlotte Islands. The closures were timed sequentially in order to shepherd endangered coho through the various fishing zones. Although many fishers bemoaned the closures, John McCulloch, vice-president of Langara Fishing Lodge Ltd., praised the moves, saying "the department of fisheries is finally making the changes they should have made 25 years ago."[15]

The DFO also announced the establishment of a new deal between U.S. and Canadian fishers, in which U.S. fishers would cut their catch of coho headed for the Upper Thompson River by 22 percent. In return, Canadian fishers would decrease their catch of United States–bound chinook by 50 percent. Each country would thus be giving up approximately 7,000 fish.

Also in June 1998, Canada suffered the embarrassment of being asked to account to the North American Free Trade Agreement's Environmental Commission for allegedly ignoring the wholesale destruction of salmon habitat.

A few weeks later, the beleaguered Canadian coho took another hit when about 3,000 juvenile coho were killed in Murray Creek near Langley, after a toxic pesticide accidentally spilled into the creek.

In late July, commercial and sport salmon fishing was closed on the Yukon and Alsek Rivers after record low returns. Chinook salmon returns in the Yukon were found to be 77 percent below normal.

Mother Nature dealt the salmon yet another blow in August 1998, when weeks of record high temperatures sent water temperatures in upriver B.C. streams soaring to the highest levels in eighty-seven years. Compounding this problem were abnormally low river levels due to low runoff following an unusually warm

The bony skeleton of this piscacarid fish makes it an excellent candidate for fossilization.

A single spawning female salmon can lay up to 20,000 eggs at one time.

Coho eggs and alevins hiding among the river's gravel bed. The large black eyes of the alevins make them sensitive to light.

A mayfly hatching swarm is an irresistible aerial buffet to young salmon.

Salmon fry will hide among aquatic plants until they are ready to move out to sea.

Because of their small size, these salmon fingerlings are vulnerable to a large variety of predators.

Two female sockeyes vying for position in the spawning gravel.

Spawning sockeye salmon swarming in Fulton River, B.C.

A male sockeye running a riffle.

A sow grizzly feasting on a chum salmon dinner.

After spawning salmon bodies litter the stream banks and become an important part of the ecological food chain.

Log booms cause a tremendous amount of bark to fall into lakes and streams. This can ultimately smother thousands of precious salmon eggs.

Pollution and the disposal of garbage in waterways continues to destroy many salmon streams.

A fish trap in the Sooke area off Vancouver Island, circa 1905.

A salmon farm in the Broughton archipelago off the B.C. coast.

winter. Water levels in the Fraser River system hit their lowest point since 1912. To further exacerbate this problem, a small amount of water will heat up faster than a large amount, which meant that the low levels of water caused temperatures to soar in Fraser River tributaries. For example, temperatures in the Horsefly River hit 70°F (21°C), ten degrees higher than the preferred water temperature for spawning sockeye. Many early-run Stuart River sockeye died from heat exhaustion before they could make it to the spawning gravels. The DFO estimated that 25 percent of the sockeye in the Fraser River system wouldn't spawn, due to the extreme heat.

Early August 1998 also saw alarmingly low sockeye returns in Alaska. Alaska governor Tony Knowles declared western Alaska a disaster area and offered $19 million in aid to financially strapped fishers and fishing communities.

In June 1999, Canada and the United States reached a comprehensive agreement under the new Pacific Salmon Treaty. Under this treaty, rules and shares of catch were set out for fourteen separate fisheries of five salmon species. The treaty established two funds totalling $209 million (Cdn.) for salmon-conservation initiatives and revised previous fishing quota systems to allow more of the threatened chinook and coho stocks through to their spawning grounds in Canada.

Barely two months later, the Fraser River sockeye fishery, the richest fishery on the continent, was closed to all fishing due to dangerously low stocks. The move was expected to mean at least $60 million in lost revenue to B.C. fishers alone.

After a hundred years of overfishing, habitat destruction, pollution and dam construction, the Pacific salmon and the people who depend upon the salmon for their living are now making a last stand. Whether they will make it or not is largely up to us....

8. THE FATE OF THE FISH

"The [fish] resource is a trust and the first responsibility of angler, manager, scientist and politician is to ensure its protection and perpetuation. Others who come after us will need it."
Roderick Haig-Brown, *Bright Waters, Bright Fish,* 1980

Much of the abuse suffered by salmon over the past century and a half can be reversed if public pressure is strong enough. As U.S. fisheries historian James McGoodwin wrote in his excellent 1990 book *Crisis in the World's Fisheries,* "marine organisms are renewable organisms...and even when they are exploited to the point of depletion, they can usually rebound if they are permitted to do so."[1]

Many factors have been involved in the decline of the Pacific salmon in North America. Biologists tend to put the largest amount of blame on ocean climate change. Others blame the hatcheries. The hatcheries blame the commercial fishers. The commercial fishers blame the Native fishers. Others blame the sport fishers. Still others blame the fish farmers. And almost everyone blames the government for bungling the management of the fishery.

In the final analysis, there have been four main factors in the decline of the Pacific salmon: habitat loss, overfishing, climate change and possibly the excessive release of too many hatchery fish into the ocean.

For all too many salmon who try to return home to spawn, the truth is there is simply no home to return to. All across the Pacific Northwest, the natural habitats of the salmon have been either damaged, diminished or destroyed. Very few residents of the posh condominiums along Puget Sound remember that, some years ago, the waters of Puget Sound were alive with spawning coho and chum salmon. But alas, no more. In many wetland areas across the West Coast, the most common sight is now the construction crane.

The most affected of all salmon have been coho, chinook and steelhead, whose numbers prove that historically they have produced far fewer fish than other species, from far fewer stocks. In addition, because all three of these species spend long periods in freshwater before going to sea, they are the main salmon species to have been hurt by the negative effects of streamside logging operations, pulp-and-paper mills, agriculture and dam construction.

Coho are especially affected by habitat loss due to their habit of spawning in small coastal streams. These streams have been hit hard by the dual threats of urban growth and resulting pollution. In addition, coho and chinook tend to travel the least distance out to sea, which means they are most likely to suffer the marine effects of coastal pollution and habitat damage.

The first step in reversing habitat loss and damage is to identify key salmon habitats. Unbelievably, it has been estimated that less than 1 percent of salmon streams in the Pacific Northwest have been catalogued. Even fewer have been accurately mapped. Many biologists have recommended to the government that a major mapping project be established to provide basic data on salmon streams.

The second step is to restore habitat, and many habitat-restoration projects are now under way. Sometimes it doesn't take much to help the salmon along. In 1984, Salmonid Enhancement Program technicians left two dumptruck-loads of gravel at the head of Worth Creek in southern British Columbia, intending to return in 1987 to work the gravel into spawning beds. The salmon beat them to it. Crews returned to find the pile of gravel gone, spread by chum and coho into a perfect spawning bed in which they had already laid their eggs.

Across the border, habitat loss and damage have yet again played prime roles in the decline of the salmon. For example, between 1920 and 1950, U.S. coho catches from the Columbia River plummeted from 4,000 tons a year to less than 500 tons due to the one-two-three punch of logging, dam building and agriculture.

Since 1980, about $100 million (U.S.) has been spent annually by American agencies to preserve and enhance the Columbia River's salmon stocks, 90 percent of which face extinction. The goal is to double the Columbia River's salmon runs to approximately 5 million fish. This number actually represents only about half the original salmon population before habitat loss took its toll, but it's a start.

OVERFISHING

Although most fishers respect fish as a resource, basic greed has raised for years its ugly head in the fishery.

In 1966, for example, the B.C. Department of Fisheries declared that 40 percent of the provincial fishing fleet could easily provide the annual catch of salmon. A pointed comment on the overcapacity of the fishing fleet in British Columbia.

All around the Pacific it is the same sad story. In many areas, the 1980s and early 1990s were boom times for fishers. The annual Korean salmon catch, for example, increased over thirty times, from an average of 90 tons between 1962 and 1971 to a peak of 2,811 tons in 1986. The number of U.S. trawling vessels fishing for herring, groundfish and shrimp in the northeast Pacific region more than quadrupled, from 36 boats in 1983 to 179 in 1991. Independent fisheries consultant David Ellis believes that the overfishing of herring, a major food for both coho and chinook, is partly to blame for the decline of those two species off the West Coast.

In 1997, the U.N. Food and Agricultural Organization estimated that 53 percent of the world's fishing fleet represented excess capacity.

There are simply too many fishers chasing far too few fish.

Most of the factors behind the decline of the salmon are attributable directly to human folly, but the byproduct of human activity known as global warming has also seriously hurt salmon stocks.

One of the world's leading authorities on Pacific salmon, Cornelis Groot, the retired head biologist at the Pacific Biological Station in Nanaimo, British Columbia, has forecast a dim future for the salmon.

Groot has predicted an increase in the average water temperature off the West Coast of several degrees over the next 50 to 100 years. The upwellings of water along the coast in summer, which bring abundant food to the surface, will decrease, he says, causing a decrease in salmon numbers. Climatic zones will shift northward, but the strong homing instinct of salmon will prevent their southern populations from moving north, and many stocks will die out. Higher temperatures will then create increases in bacterial infections and parasitic infestations.

In 1990, a team of biologists searched the North Pacific Ocean in winter and found no salmon south of the 45°F (7°C) isotherm. "It was like a wall in the ocean," biologist David Welch said. "On one side there's salmon, and on the other side, there's not."[2]

Salmon most likely remain in colder water in order to conserve their energy. Salmon are a cold-blooded species, whose bodies assume the approximate temperature of the surrounding water. Warm water temperatures can cause fish to lose more energy than they gain from feeding, and thus they slowly starve. The 45°F (7°C) isotherm is therefore likely a temperature barrier beyond which salmon simply can't survive.

But what happens if the North Pacific waters heat up as a result of global warming? If carbon dioxide levels double, as some scientists are predicting, and the planet warms as a result, the temperature barrier for salmon in winter will move far north, to just south of the Alaskan coast. In summer, the barrier could move north of Alaska, to the Bering Sea. The salmon would simply disappear from all the southern parts of their present range.

Recent Far North fish catches may prove to be evidence of a northward shift in some salmon populations. In the fall of 1998, twelve chum were caught by fishers in nets at the mouth of the

The Fate of the Fish

Mackenzie River, far north of the fish's normal range. In addition, biologists studying whitefish in the Peel River, a tributary of the Mackenzie River, were surprised to catch more than forty chum.

The salmon of the Adams River are also in considerable danger from global warming. Since 1959, the average temperature of the river has increased by 1.5 degrees. A 1992 study of the river by biologists Michael Henderson and John Stockner warned of reduced food for juvenile sockeyes as a result of warming, and concluded: "The rapid increase in temperature anticipated over the next 50 to 150 years will almost certainly...lead to a decrease in growth and survival."[3] According to the Oregon Fish Commission, if the temperature of the Columbia River increases just 5.4 degrees, the remaining chinook runs there will *all* become extinct.

Added to the long-term general climatic change are the short-term effects of such climate anomalies as El Niños. Normally, trade winds blow from east to west along the equator, and the air pushes a warm layer of surface water to the west toward Asia. El Niño years see a reversal of this trend; the winds blow from west to east, pushing a bulge of warm water to the east, toward North America. The effect occurs at roughly five-year intervals, for reasons still unknown.

The most recent major El Niño took place in late 1982 and early 1983, an event which has been called the largest climate anomaly of the twentieth century. A less intense El Niño occurred in 1997–98, but, even during this lesser event, sea-surface temperatures off many parts of the West Coast were two to four degrees above normal.

Young coho are particularly susceptible to temperature increases; when sea-surface temperatures abruptly increased in 1977, coho smolt survival took a nose dive. Coho growth is also affected; the average size of coho caught in 1983, after the 1982–83 El Niño, was the smallest on record to that date.

Biologists have found that, in El Niño years, warm-water predators such as large Pacific mackerel (normally only found south of the California–Oregon border) appear, and predation upon salmon increases. During the minor El Niño of 1991–92, mackerel caught in Barkley Sound on the west coast of Vancouver Island typically each had six to eight juvenile salmon in their stomachs. In 1992 and 1993, mackerel killed up to 90 percent of the young salmon off the west coast of Vancouver Island.

Another warm-water resident is the hake. One published estimate suggested that a temperature increase of only one degree centigrade could double the number of hake in Canadian waters. By late 1997, the hake population in the Strait of Georgia indeed had more than doubled. And since hake eat the same foods as young coho and chinooks, the salmon fishery suffers as a result.

An El Niño also causes a shift in salmon migration. During El Niño years, many salmon use a route north of Vancouver Island through Johnstone Strait instead of their normal route south of the island through the Juan de Fuca Strait. This shift can destroy the accuracy of run estimations, leading to massive overfishing.

El Niños create a higher air pressure off the west coast, decreasing the upwelling of cold, deep, nutrient-rich water. These upwellings play a crucial role in the marine survival of coho during the summer of smolt migration. In one 1986 study, the survival of hatchery coho smolts in strong upwelling years was about twice that in weak years. It is thought that, with strong upwellings, there is more food, faster growth, and reduced predation due to both the increased size of the salmon and their increased dispersal. It is also possible that upwellings transport smolts farther offshore, beyond the reach of inshore predators. With weak upwellings, smolts stay in the narrow zone of upwelled water close to shore, where numerous hungry predators lurk.

In addition, El Niños affect the timing of the plankton blooms that feed young salmon when they first enter the ocean. It has been found, for example, that the density of plankton is reduced by up to 70 percent in El Niño years due to the dampening effect on ocean upwellings. The reduced volume of plankton is thought to cause major declines in salmon populations.

The warmer water brought with El Niños also increases the number of "red tide" algal infestations, which can kill salmon. Many marine diseases reproduce more rapidly in warm water.

And finally, in El Niño years, less snow falls, leading to a smaller spring runoff and lower water levels in the major salmon rivers and their tributaries. Salmon smolts depend on high spring water levels to help carry them to the sea.

Recent years have seen a great deal of research into the links between climate and fish production. In 1993, Fisheries biologists announced that an important measurable link between climate and salmon survival had been found. They discovered that the Aleutian Low Pressure Index, which measures the intensity of winter low pressure in the subarctic Pacific Ocean, bears a close relationship with catches of pink, chum and sockeye.

In a normal winter, low pressure in the North Pacific pushes water inland. When the swells reach the coast, cool, nutrient-rich water from below is pushed to the surface. Plankton feed on the nutrients, small fish feed on the plankton, and salmon feed on the small fish. But when the Aleutian Low becomes weak, there is less turbulent water, and ultimately less food for salmon. Fewer salmon survive to maturity, and fewer are caught.

In 1998, a number of scientists hit the headlines with their research into the ties between climate and salmon production.

In January, B.C. biologist Carl Walters announced his findings that salmon appear to be on the decline globally, and not just on the west coast of North America. He found that, for salmon spawning in the Miramichi River and other eastern rivers, the ocean survival rate has dropped to less than 2 percent. At that level, stocks cannot replace themselves. In the 1970s, marine survival rates for Strait of Georgia coho averaged 12 to 15 percent; by 1997, survival had decreased to 2 to 5 percent. Walters found that the declines of Pacific salmon, which started about 1985, were almost perfectly mirrored by similar declines of the Atlantic salmon at about the same time. "The only thing on this scale," he says, "is global warming."[4]

In July, John McGowan of California's Scripps Institution of Oceanography published an article in the journal *Science*, stating that a general warming trend over the past twenty years has had a profound effect on marine life. McGowan studied sea-surface temperatures along the west coast of North America from 1916 on and found that the entire system had warmed up. Since 1977, sea-surface temperatures have stayed an average of two degrees above normal. The results have been similar to those due to El Niños: a general decline in zooplankton, the microscopic life that is the base of the marine food chain; the appearance of warm-water predators far north of their normal range; the blocking of upwellings of nutrient-rich cold water by warm surface water; and a change in salt content of the ocean water. All of these have had negative effects on the salmon fishery. McGowan says the changes are consistent with global warming.

In August, Howard Freeland, head of the DFO's Pacific region ocean science and productivity division, announced that "this year, for the first time [in forty-two years] we saw no detectable nutrients in the surface waters [off the B.C. coast] in June."[5] Since plankton feed on those nutrients, and salmon feed on the plankton, his finding meant even more bad news for the salmon.

Normally, nutrients churned up from deep water last through the summer. But, for some reason, the nutrients are now running out sooner. The decline is, so far, confined to an area that stretches 500 miles (805 km) offshore. Although many salmon spend their time further offshore, coho and chinook are common in this area. And all salmon must pass through the low-nutrient area on their way back to spawn. With less food, fewer salmon are going to make it to their spawning grounds.

Freeland suspects "it is probably a global warming problem,"[6] but admits that ocean climate changes are a complex topic, requiring years of data collection and analysis.

Clearly, much research remains to be done in this crucial area, for if biologists can predict future warming trends and arrival dates of El Niños, they can more accurately recommend sustainable catch quotas. And that would go a long way to help Pacific salmon recover their lost numbers.

EXCESSIVE HATCHERY RELEASES

Some biologists wonder if the billions of hatchery fish released into the Pacific Ocean each year may be overloading the system, leading to increased competition for food, and ultimately the starvation of many salmon. Each year over 5 billion hatchery fish are released by Canada, Japan, the United States and the Russian Federation, including approximately 300 million chinook and 113 million coho.

The problem is that no one can exactly determine what the carrying capacity of the ocean is. Theoretically, overstocking of the ocean might lead to generally smaller fish, due to increased competition for food. There is some evidence of this.

Many countries have reported a general decline in the size of pinks, the species that has been released in greatest numbers. At the Kitoi Bay hatchery in Alaska, the average size of returning pinks decreased from 3.3–3.5 pounds (1.5–1.6 kg) in the early 1980s to 3.1 pounds (1.4 kg) in 1989–90, after hatchery releases that were increased from 23 million to 90 million.[7]

In 1994, American biologists John H. Helle and Brian Bigler studied forty-seven runs of pink, sockeye, chum, coho and chinook and found that forty-five of them showed a decline in the average weight of the fish. In nine of the runs, the average weight had dropped by as much as 25 percent since the 1970s.

Japan reported recently that in their 1997 catch, the average size of sockeye and chum were both below the six-year averages of 1991 through 1996.[8]

But such decreases have not been reported for all stocks, and other factors such as climate changes or decreases in food sources have probably played important roles in the size of the fish. This makes it difficult to focus blame for this problem exclusively on the hatcheries.

What we know to be of concern, however, is the huge cost of producing 5 billion hatchery fish annually. Many biologists believe that the hundreds of millions of dollars spent on hatchery programs around the Pacific could be better spent on conserving or restoring salmon habitat.

SAVING THE SALMON

The real challenge for salmon-fishery managers today is to enact conservation measures that minimize negative impacts on fishery stakeholders and on fishery-dependent communities while maximizing benefits to the salmon.

Recently, fishers off the West Coast of Canada screamed loud and long when it was announced that tough fishery restrictions would continue well into the next decade. But without that long-term rationalization, there literally is no future for the salmon fisher. Better conservation today means better long-run profits tomorrow and allows more people in the future to partake in the fishery. Many of the younger fishers seeking temporary work outside the fishery now may well return later after the current crisis has eased.

Many forms of aid to salmon fishers exist. In Canada's most recent aid package for the salmon industry, a $100-million fund was set aside to help older fishers retire early, to retrain fishers for work outside the fishery and to help communities decrease their dependance on salmon fishing. In Seattle, $255 million (U.S.) has been earmarked for restoration of ruined salmon runs, with part of those funds going to displaced salmon fishers, who will provide some of the labor for restoring the salmon runs.

Other displaced salmon fishers could redirect their efforts toward catching only healthy stocks or fishing in areas where accidental by-catches of threatened stocks are minimized. Kathy Scarfo, president of the West Coast Salmon Trollers' Association, agrees with this alternative, stating specifically that her group would "like to fish in areas where there is less coho sensitivity."[9]

There is unfortunately no question that the conservation approach to salmon management does have human costs in the short term. All fishery managers can hope for is to minimize those costs wherever possible so that the long-term gains will outweigh the costs.

So, keeping the human costs in mind, what is needed today to save the Pacific salmon? A ten-step program can be recommended.

1. Restore salmon habitat.

The most serious problem affecting wildlife the world over is habitat loss. Along the West Coast, additional efforts must be made to identify, preserve and restore salmon habitat. Instead of spending hundreds of millions of dollars on direct aid and unemployment payments to displaced fishers, perhaps the money could be better spent employing these people to work on salmon-habitat restoration and conservation.

Some fishers have already joined conservation projects. Veteran fisher Alan Moore voluntarily tied up his boat to help map Vancouver Island salmon streams. "This should have been done years ago," he says. "How can you protect or rehabilitate [salmon] habitat when you don't know where it is? We've found salmon in streams no one knew produced salmon. We've found streams no one knew about."[10]

2. Decrease the overcapacity of the fishing fleet.

The number of fishing boats in the salmon fleet must be decreased further in order to decrease overfishing of the remaining resource. Of additional concern is the concentration of the fishing in the hands of major corporations, which return few benefits to the local fishing communities. Some of the large commercial boat owners have international operations. If one fishery is depleted, they just move elsewhere. Local fishers are the big losers.

3. Reduce fishing for coho until stocks rebound.

The Canadian ban on coho fishing must be continued until coho stocks increase to levels that can be harvested in a sustainable manner. Many biologists have recommended that a total ban on commercial and recreational coho fishing in California, Oregon and Washington also be put in place, and that no coho fishing be allowed to resume until coho stocks at least double. Coho numbers in Alaska are still quite healthy.

4. Enact a ban on chinook fishing in Canada.

The recommendation of many biologists to close the Canadian chinook fishery until stocks build up seems to make sense. Biologist Carl Walters has noted that "chinook salmon collapse in the Georgia Strait was first predicted in about 1979, and we still have not taken the obvious steps needed to reverse that."[11] Although commercial gillnetting for chinook was closed down in the lower Fraser River in the 1980s, a much more widespread closure is necessary. Despite all the press about the decline of the coho, the Canadian chinook catch has actually seen a larger decline from historic levels.

Across the border, chinook catches in California, Oregon and Washington are about half of what they used to be. While a complete ban on chinook fishing in those states is probably not required, additional restrictions would be a welcome conservation measure. Chinook catches in Alaska are relatively healthy.

Strong lobbying from the sport-fishing community has helped to keep the chinook fishery open on both sides of the border, for many an angler longs to match muscle with the largest of salmon, but chinook stocks are so low now that a more far-sighted attitude on the part of these fishers is needed.

5. *Fund additional research and improve education.*
There must be additional and intensive research into salmon biology and management, especially the effects of climate change on the fishery. In fact, an international effort on the part of the five North Pacific nations is needed now before the North Pacific fishery gets any closer to collapsing.

In big-game management, a license surcharge is used to help finance scientific research; the same idea could be used to fund research into the crucial links between ocean climate change and the productivity of the ocean.

And there is a great need to disseminate the results of that research, better educating the public, the fishers and the politicians about salmon biology and salmon management. Theoretically at least, if everyone is better informed, the salmon will be better managed.

6. *Develop more selective fishing techniques.*
A serious problem in fishery management today is the amount of by-catch—the amount of unwanted species of fish caught in nets or on lines. For example, during the fall, gillnet catches for chum will bring in thousands of endangered steelhead and chinook as well. Almost all die as a result.

In the U.S. Juan de Fuca Strait fishery alone, the by-catch of coho salmon during sockeye, pink and chum fisheries between 1987 and 1992 averaged a staggering 160,000 coho per year and about 16,000 chinook per year.

And it is not only the salmon fishers who are to blame. Hake trawlers in the Strait of Juan de Fuca also take thousands of by-caught salmon each year. During the 1983 hake fishery, more than 6,000 endangered chinook were taken.

Understandably, fishers are loathe to admit that they've accidentally caught and killed thousands of endangered fish, and many instances of inaccurate record-keeping do exist. In 1991, the DFO was given statistics that stated that 1,407 coho and 10 steelhead had been caught during three chum gillnet openings in the Nitinat chum fishery off Vancouver Island. An investigation by fisheries biologist Rob Bison, however, determined that the numbers were actually 3,790 coho and 236 steelhead, more than double the numbers reported.[12]

New methods of selective harvesting have recently been tried, such as requiring seiners to "braile" their catch, using handheld dipnets to release coho; having gillnetters "hot pick," checking their nets at least every thirty minutes to cut down on the number of coho that accidentally drown in the nets; and asking trollers not to put hooks on the first 60 feet (18 m) of lines to avoid coho, which swim near the surface. Trollers in British Columbia also are now required to use barbless hooks and release each coho caught.

7. *Divert funds from hatcheries to habitat restoration and ocean climate research.*

When economist Peter Pearse reviewed fifteen years of work by Canada's Salmonid Enhancement Program, he was very critical of the money spent on hatcheries. He stated in his 1994 report that wild salmon stocks in some cases had been "displaced and replaced by enhanced stocks,"[13] hardly the original intent.

Similarly, American biologist Gary K. Meffe wrote in the September 1992 issue of *Conservation Biology* of his findings that hatcheries tend to divert government dollars away from efforts at restoring salmon habitats, tend to encourage high non-sustainable harvest rates, and ultimately can cause a decline in the abundance of wild salmon populations.

Many biologists have recommended that some of the millions of dollars spent on hatcheries be diverted elsewhere, such as to habitat restoration and ocean-climate research. Habitat restoration probably would be the best recipient of these funds. As Guido Rahr, a spokesman for the fish conservation group Oregon Trout, says, "the safest, most reliable, most productive and most inexpensive hatchery of all is a healthy river and its native stocks of salmon and steelhead."[14]

8. *Consider an end to centralized state fishery management.*

In 1995, the David Suzuki Foundation published an interesting paper entitled "Fisheries that Work—Sustainability through Community-Based Management." The paper was written by Evelyn Pinkerton, a marine anthropologist, and Martin Weinstein, a Natural Resources scientist. The two studied fisheries management systems around the world and determined that successful sustainable fisheries occurred when people involved in the fishery had a strong say in the management of their fishery.

In eastern Canada, many fishery managers believe that Atlantic cod stocks began to decline only when huge offshore fleets of boats controlled by large corporations entered the fishery. Prior to that, they argue, the small community-based inshore fishers regulated themselves quite well and comprised a sustainable fishery. Today, other groups such as the Kuskokwim Working Group in Alaska and the Skeena Watershed Committee in British Columbia are providing useful input to the management of their fisheries, a concept that is worth expanding throughout the Pacific salmon fishery. As commercial fisher John Stevens says, "if the communities were allowed to sit down and work things out, we'd be a lot better off."[15]

9. *Protect genetic diversity through a gene bank.*

In resource management, it is always wise to develop a worst-case scenario and provide for it accordingly. In the case of the Pacific salmon, it makes sense now to gather the genetic material of some of the most endangered stocks and preserve them for possible reintroduction later. A *Jurassic Park* scenario, but with a happy ending.

Since the 1980s, scientists with the World Fisheries Trust and the International Fisheries Gene Bank have worked together to preserve such genetic material. In the 1990s, their attention focused on the plight of the Pacific salmon. Genetic material from a number of threatened stocks has now been frozen for future use. But material from many other stocks needs to be added.

The problem is, however, that these efforts rely on the hope that salmon habitats will exist in the future in which to reintroduce a stock....

The Fate of the Fish

...And so I would like to offer one final recommendation. After many years as a naturalist, I have learned that the only way to truly protect an endangered space or species is to give it full legal protection. As habitat loss has played a major role in decreasing salmon stocks, I believe that the time is right for setting aside crucial salmon-spawning streams as completely protected Salmon Conservation Areas, within which there is no fishing allowed, and as little human activity as possible.

The next generation may well never see salmon runs like the one I watched in the golden autumn of 1998 in places like the Adams River. And what a loss that would be.

Future generations deserve the right to stroll along the rivers; hear the sigh of the winds through the valleys; and see thousands of sparkling fish gathered in the cold, clear water. We envy their beauty, we are awed by their strength and we admire the wonder of it all.

After watching the miracle of the Adams River salmon run, I would often think how wonderful it would be to forever preserve some of the other prime salmon habitats across North America: the Kenai, Brooks and Situk Rivers in Alaska; the Babine, Campbell, Skeena and Horsefly Rivers in British Columbia. The Klamath. The Deschutes. The Umpqua. What an incredible difference these areas could make to the future of the Pacific salmon if they were all preserved as protected areas.

And what an incredible legacy they would be for us all.

APPENDIX

The Geological Time Scale

Period	Millions of Years Ago
Quaternary	2
Tertiary	66
Cretaceous	144
Jurassic	208
Triassic	245
Permian	286
Carboniferous	360
Devonian	408
Silurian	438
Ordovician	505
Cambrian	570
PreCambrian	4,500

APPENDIX B

TABLE 1. British Columbia Commercial and Sport Catch of Salmon, 1985–1997

	Chinook	Sockeye	Coho	Pink	Chum
1985	1,126,186	12,219,368	3,676,842	20,315,665	5,470,540
1986	1,008,229	10,548,934	5,478,453	17,980,763	5,580,626
1987	925,215	5,398,109	4,012,884	13,428,904	2,270,411
1988	877,571	4,464,278	3,828,020	23,123,829	6,172,067
1989	835,373	13,755,682	3,964,394	17,163,377	1,816,809
1990	846,205	14,206,509	4,513,624	17,264,620	3,206,951
1991	846,638	10,439,390	3,738,712	24,261,157	2,354,759
1992	863,798	8,290,072	3,635,722	10,321,558	4,012,717
1993	808,843	18,110,008	2,738,623	10,262,985	4,132,995
1994	501,918	11,584,871	2,860,607	2,225,954	4,326,942
1995	378,758	4,496,908	2,139,968	12,069,224	2,469,121
1996	251,016	5,797,562	1,726,480	5,939,385	1,350,411
1997	269,487	10,696,630	334,141	6,610,086	1,890,281

(Source: Department of Fisheries and Oceans)

APPENDIX C

TABLE 2. Alaska Commercial and Sport Catch, 1985–1997

	Chinook	Sockeye	Coho	Pink	Chum
1985	811,718	39,155,630	5,949,777	90,473,297	10,586,539
1986	721,482	32,394,448	6,548,887	77,465,960	12,536,725
1987	796,402	36,909,243	3,728,435	46,612,070	10,592,787
1988	723,452	30,329,067	4,754,450	50,14,759	15,149,029
1989	694,737	44,575,871	4,988,195	97,033,778	7,930,647
1990	789,908	53,932,118	5,803,936	88,210,056	8,024,525
1991	763,420	44,973,047	6,542,569	128,487,316	9,787,209
1992	759,919	58,655,752	7,440,516	60,746,372	10,240,299
1993	877,333	64,597,661	6,462,487	109,755,582	12,258,519
1994	816,870	53,067,605	10,053,127	116,864,140	16,156,877
1995	819,507	63,769,230	6,839,631	128,455,324	18,822,646
1996	621,307	50,265,533	6,333,413	98,060,623	21,272,091
1997	835,463	31,252,841	3,362,931	71,385,745	15,644,157

(Source: Alaska Department of Fish and Game)

APPENDIX D

TABLE 3. California, Oregon and Washington Ocean Commercial Troll and Recreational Catch, 1985–1998

	Chinook	Coho	Pink
1985	884,000	679,000	170,000
1986	1,461,000	1,049,000	0
1987	1,773,000	888,000	41,000
1988	2,121,000	1,098,000	0
1989	1,196,000	1,179,000	55,000
1990	915,000	851,000	0
1991	528,000	1,061,000	52,000
1992	444,000	466,000	0
1993	546,000	291,000	8,000
1994	515,000	500	0
1995	1,311,000	138,000	45,000
1996	729,000	95,000	500
1997	899,000	45,000	3,000
1998	488,000	31,000	0

NOTE: Catches of sockeye and chum are rare in ocean fisheries in California, Oregon and Washington and are not recorded.

(Source: Pacific Fishery Management Council)

NOTES

CHAPTER 1: THE SPIRIT OF THE PACIFIC
1. Mark Hume, *Adam's River: The Mystery of the Adams River Sockeye* (Vancouver: New Star Books, 1994).
2. "U.S. sets stiff rules to save fish runs," *Vancouver Sun*, March 17, 1999, p. A6.
3. David Anderson, "No pain, no gain: Putting the fish first," *Vancouver Sun*, July 18, 1998, p. A23.

CHAPTER 2: A FAMILY OF FISH
1. Personal communication dated June 20, 1997, with Sergey Kurayev, of the Russian Ministry of Protection of the Environment and Natural Resources.

CHAPTER 4: THE SALMON LIFE CYCLE: BORN TO DIE
1. William G. Pearcy, *Ocean Ecology of North Pacific Salmonids* (Seattle: University of Washington Press, 1992), p. 1.
2. Erich Hoyt, *Orca: The Whale Called Killer* (Camden East, ON: Camden House, 1981), p. 63.
3. Ibid., p. 161.
4. Michael E. Long, "Secrets of animal navigation," *National Geographic*, 179/6 (June 1991): 89.

CHAPTER 5: OF FISH AND MEN
1. Roderick Haig-Brown, *Bright Water, Bright Fish* (Vancouver: Douglas & McIntyre, 1980), p. 63.
2. Jere Van Dyk, "Long journey of the Pacific Salmon," *National Geographic*, 178/1 (July 1990): 27.

3. W.E. Ricker, "Effects of the fishery and of obstacles to migration on the abundance of Fraser River sockeye salmon. Technical Report," *Fisheries & Aquatic Sciences* 1522 (1987).

CHAPTER 6: TO SAVE THE SALMON
1. Internal Report on Fort Alexandria by Chief Trader Joseph McGillivray, 1827: Hudson's Bay Company Archives.
2. Rebecca J. Goldburg, "Benefits and risks of a growing aquaculture industry," *EDF Letter* [Washington, D.C.: Environmental Defense Fund], 27/1 (January 1996): 7.

CHAPTER 7: A HISTORY OF SALMON FISHING IN NORTH AMERICA
1. H.H. Bancroft, *The Works of H.H. Bancroft*. Vol. 30: *History of Oregon, 1848–1888* (San Francisco: H.H. Bancroft, 1888), p. 758.
2. Wilmot Royal Commission, Sessional Papers, 1893: National Archives of Canada.
3. R.D. Hume, *Salmon of the Pacific Coast* (San Francisco: Schmidt Label & Lithographic, 1893).
4. First and Second Annual Reports of the Fish and Game Protector to the Governor, 1893–1894, pp. 7–8.
5. Livingstone Stone, *Explorations on the Columbia River from the Head of Clarke's Fork to the Pacific Ocean, Made in the Summer of 1883, with Reference to the Selection of a Suitable Place for Establishing a Salmon Breeding Station* (Washington, D.C.: Government Printing Office, 1885), p. 6.
6. Anon., *The Oregon Sportsman*, January 1914, p. 1.
7. Canadian Fisheries Act (1932), Clause 42, Section 1.
8. Richard L. Neuberger, "Climb, fish, climb." *Collier's*, November 6, 1937, p. 50.
9. Supreme Court Decision: *Udall* vs. *Federal Power Commission* 387 U.S. 428, 1967.
10. Supreme Court Decision: *Washington* vs. *Passenger Fishing Vessel Association* 443 U.S. 658, 1979.
11. U.S. Magnuson Fishery Conservation and Management Act, 16th U.S. Congress, 1976.
12. Northwest Power Act, 96th U.S. Congress, Second Session, 1980.
13. Gordon Hamilton, "Strips won't save salmon, lobby charges," *Vancouver Sun*, June 17, 1994, p. D1.
14. Ibid.
15. Mark Hume, "Feds slash salmon catch: Industry put on $400 million life support," *Vancouver Sun*, June 20, 1998, p. A2.

CHAPTER 8: THE FATE OF THE FISH

1. James R. McGoodwin, *Crisis in the World's Fisheries* (Stanford, Calif.: Stanford University Press, 1990).

2. "Cold comfort for salmon," *The Province*, May 28, 1998, p. A11.

3. Hume, Mark, *Adam's River: The Mystery of the Adams River Sockeye* (Vancouver: New Star Books, 1994).

4. Hume, Mark. "Salmon decline worldwide, expert says," *Vancouver Sun*, January 27, 1998, p. B5.

5. Tom Barrett, "Warm seas ruining B.C. fishery," *Vancouver Sun*, August 15, 1998, p. A1.

6. Ibid.

7. William G. Pearcy, *Ocean Ecology of North American Salmonids* (Seattle: University of Washington Press, 1992), p. 103.

8. *North Pacific Anadromous Fish Commission 1997 Report.* (Vancouver, 1998), p. 30.

9. Jim Beatty and Jeff Lee, "B.C. groups disagree on how to save coho," *Vancouver Sun*, June 17, 1997, p. A1.

10. "They're mapping the future," *The Province*, August 9, 1998, p. A25.

11. Carl Walters, *Fish on the Line: The Future of Pacific Fisheries* (Vancouver: David Suzuki Foundation, 1995).

12. R.G. Bison, "The interception of steelhead, chinook and coho salmon during three commercial gillnet openings at Nitinat, 1991." Report for the Ministry of Environment, Lands, and Parks; Fisheries Branch, 1993.

13. Peter Pearse, "An assessment of the salmon stock development program on Canada's West Coast," Vancouver: Program Review of the Salmonid Enhancement Program, Internal Audits and Evaluations Branch, Department of Fisheries and Oceans, 1994.

14. Guido Rahr, "Are hatchery fish the answer for the future?" *Salmon Trout Steelheader* 30/1 (August/September 1996): 11.

15. Terry Glavin, *Dead Reckoning: Confronting the Crisis in Pacific Fisheries* (Vancouver: Douglas & McIntyre, 1996), p. 130.

BIBLIOGRAPHY

Anderson, Charlie. "Creek turns deadly." *The Province*, July 27, 1998, pp. A1–2.

Anderson, David. "No pain, no gain: putting fish first." *Vancouver Sun*, July 18, 1998, p. A23.

Andrews, Ralph W., and A.K. Larssen. *Fish and Ships*. New York: Bonanza Books, 1992.

Ball, Gordon. *Pacific Salmon: From Egg to Exit*. Surrey, B.C.: Hancock House, 1996.

Barrett, Tom. "Warm seas ruining B.C. fishery." *Vancouver Sun*, August 15, 1998, pp. A1, A18.

British Columbia Freshwater Fishing Regulations, 1997–1998. Victoria: Ministry of Environment, Lands and Parks—Fisheries Branch.

Childerhouse, R.J., and Marj Trim. *Pacific Salmon and Steelhead Trout*. Vancouver: Douglas and McIntyre, 1979.

Cone, Joseph, and Sandy Ridlington, eds. *The Northwest Salmon Crisis: A Documentary History*. Corvallis, OR: Oregon State University Press, 1996.

Copes, Parzival. "Coping with the Coho crisis." *The Western Fisherman* 12/12 (June 1998): 23–32.

Dangers to Salmonids. Salmonid Enhancement Program Fact Sheet. Ottawa: Department of Fisheries and Oceans, nd.

DFO Factbook. Ottawa: Department of Fisheries and Oceans, 1993.

Fish News: Towards a Sustainable Fishery. Victoria: Ministry of Agriculture, Fisheries and Food, December 1997.

Glavin, Terry. *Dead Reckoning: Confronting the Crisis in Pacific Fisheries.* Vancouver: Douglas & McIntyre, 1996.

Glossop, Jennifer, ed. *The Nature of Fish.* Toronto: Natural Science of Canada Limited, 1974.

Goldburg, Rebecca J. "Benefits and risks of a growing aquaculture industry." *EDF Letter* [Washington, D.C.: Environmental Defense Fund] 27/1 (January 1996): 7.

Groot, Cornelis, and Leo Margolis, eds. *Pacific Salmon Life Histories.* Vancouver: University of British Columbia Press, 1991.

Homolka, Kenneth, and Timothy W. Downey. "Assessment of thermal effects on salmon spawning and fry emergence, Upper McKenzie River, 1992." *Information Reports, No. 95-4.* Portland, OR: Oregon Department of Fish and Wildlife, 1995.

Hume, Mark. *Adam's River: The Mystery of the Adams River Sockeye.* Vancouver: New Star Books, 1994.

———. "Fate of the Strait." *Vancouver Sun,* June 5, 1998, pp. 7–8.

———. *Run of the River.* Vancouver: New Star Books, 1992.

Hume, Stephen. "Fishing Alaska." *Vancouver Sun,* July 4, 1998, pp. G1–2.

The Incredible Salmonids. Ottawa: Department of Fisheries and Oceans, nd.

International North Pacific Fisheries Commission Statistical Yearbook 1992. Vancouver, 1996.

Iwamoto, Robert N., and Stacia Sower, eds. *Salmonid Reproduction: An International Symposium.* Seattle: University of Washington Press, 1985.

Jones, Bob. "Rethinking saltwater management." *B.C. Outdoors* 54/4 (May 1998): 22–23.

Keller, Betty C., and Rosella M. Leslie. *Sea-Silver.* Victoria, B.C.: Horsdal and Schubert, 1996.

Ludvigsen, Rolf, ed. *Life in Stone: A Natural History of British Columbia's Fossils.* Vancouver: University of British Columbia Press, 1996.

McKervill, Hugh W. *The Salmon People.* Vancouver: Whitecap Books, 1967.

Meggs, Geoff. *Salmon: The Decline of the B.C. Fishery.* Vancouver: Douglas & McIntyre, 1991.

Morrow, James E. *The Freshwater Fishes of Alaska.* Anchorage: Alaska Northwest Publishing, 1980.

1995 Record Book. Hayward, Wisc.: National Fresh Water Fishing Hall of Fame.

North Pacific Anadromous Fish Commission Annual Report, 1997. Vancouver, 1998.

Pearcy, William G. *Ocean Ecology of North Pacific Salmonids.* Seattle: University of Washington Press, 1992.

"Phantom of the Ocean: The Mystery of Global Climate Change." CBC Television Production, 1997.

Poole, Eric. "The salmon wars." *Vancouver Sun*, July 25, 1998, p. A21.

Reisner, Marc. "Coming undammed." *Audubon*, 100/5 (September–October 1998): 58–65.

Roderick Haig-Brown Provincial Park. Victoria: Ministry of Environment, Lands, and Parks. nd.

"Salmon fishing closed in Yukon due to low returns." *Vancouver Sun*, July 25, 1998, p. B3.

"U.S. salmon seasons cut." *The Province*, April 14, 1997, p. A20.

Walker, Robert L., and J. Scott Foott. "Disease survey of Klamath River salmonid smolt populations." *U.S. Fish and Wildlife Service 1992 Reports.* Anderson, Calif.: U.S. Fish & Wildlife Service California-Nevada Fish Health Center, 1992.

Wooding, Frederick H. *Lake, River and Sea-Run Fishes of Canada.* Madeira Park, B.C.: Harbour Publishing, 1994.

PHOTO CREDITS

Photo Insert One:

(in order of appearance)

Robert H. Busch, K.Y.K. Wong, Mark Conlin, K.Y.K. Wong, K.Y.K. Wong, Robert H. Busch, James R. Page, Don Roberts, Robert H. Busch, Graham Osborne, Robert H. Busch, Graham Osborne, Graham Osborne, Adrian Dorst.

Photo Insert Two:

(in order of appearance)

Robert H. Busch, Courtesy The Department of Fisheries and Oceans, K.Y.K. Wong, Robert McCaw, Robert H. Busch, Myron Kozak/The Driftwood Foundation, Robert H. Busch, Myron Kozak/The Driftwood Foundation, Graham Osborne, Robert McCaw, Robert H. Busch, Robert H. Busch, Robert H. Busch, B.C. Archives/B-0631, B.C. Salmon Farmers Association.

INDEX

Index